Taiji Qigong

The Energetic Foundation of Taijiquan

Dennis Sharp

Cover Photo: Hxdylzj/Ktsharp733|Dreamstime.com

Readers Please Note:

The study of the internal arts and its associated energy work (Qigong) may not be appropriate for everyone. There may be some degree of risk involved in practicing the mediation, movements, and applications presented in this book without the guidance of a qualified instructor. The information presented in this book was never intended, nor should be substituted in any way with the advice, or counseling of any licensed professional healthcare provider. It is always wise to first consult with your healthcare provider before beginning any new exercise program (especially the study of the martial arts or its associated Qigong) in order to reduce the chance of any possible injury or emotional distress. Any injury or distress from any exercise program should not be ignored and should immediately be brought to the attention of your healthcare provider.

The publisher and author of this book disclaim any liabilities for any injuries or loss in connection with following any of the practices described in this book. Any implementation of these practices is at the discretion and risk of the reader.

Table of Contents

Preface

Taiji Qigong: The Energetic Foundation of Taijiquan is a distillation of my thirty plus years of study and practice experience in the Chinese martial arts and its related energy work (Qigong). I felt that after so many years of dedicated study and teaching of the subject the time was right to pass on some of my knowledge and insights to my students as well other people who would like to learn more about the the many benefits of Taiji Qigong practice.

Taijiquan and Qigong share ancient roots that have only recently (within the last 30 years or so) become known and practiced in the west. Both Taijiquan and Qigong are based on the same philosophical principles found in the ancient Chinese classics such as in the Book of Changes (Yijing) (H. Ni) and the Yellow Emperor's Classic of Internal Medicine (Huang Di Neijing) (M. Ni). In fact Taijiquan is actually a form of movement Qigong that has been expanded into a system of personal energy cultivation and self-defense.

Acknowledgements

Thanks to my wonderful wife Kathleen for her love, encouragement and her technical assistance with the editing, illustrations and production of this publication.

Thanks to my former teachers: Sifu John S.S. Leong and the Sihings, and Sijehs (elder brothers and sisters) of the Seattle Kung Fu Club; Shifu Andrew Dale who inspired me to pursue the internal arts; the late Sensi Dave Harris who opened my eyes to all the possibilities within the Taijiquan system; Dr. Wang Xue Zhi whose teaching profoundly influenced every aspect of my teaching and personal development; I also wish to acknowledge Master Ni Hua-ching and his sons Dr. Ni Mao-shing and Ni Dao-shing as well as Dr. Yang Zwing-ming for their many publications, video tapes, and DVDs that added so much to my understanding and personal development. Thanks to my editors/students Rebecca Hershey, Gary Jones, and Rick Angel for their help and encouragement in making this publication possible. Thanks to Susie Wind for the illustrations. And lastly, a special thanks to all my students past and present for their support and encouragement.

In parting, I wish all of you the very best in your life journeys.

Shifu Dennis

Chapter 1

History of Taiji Qigong

In earlier times Taiji Qigong training was taught to a very select few individuals and its methods were closely guarded secrets. The students fortunate enough to have Qigong included in their training regimen realized that their Taijiquan skills were exponentially superior to the students who lacked this type of training.

With the advent of the Chinese Cultural Revolution (1966-1976) the Chinese Communist Party (CCP) instituted the policy that all of the ancient traditional teachings (which included the martial arts) were to be censored or suppressed. The consequences of this policy resulted in many of China's intellectuals and artists leaving China to settle and begin sharing their knowledge with other cultures all over the world. It was during this period (particularly during the 1970s) that Taijiquan and its Qigong methods were introduced to the US and Canada and began growing in popularity. I was indeed fortunate to have been given the opportunity to study with some of these esteemed Chinese masters whose teaching methods and philosophies inspired me to make teaching the art of Taijiquan and its related energy work my life's work.

There are many styles of Taijiquan and all have their merits. This book will not emphasize any one particular style but instead focus on presenting students with the fundamental energy work that may be applied to all the styles of Taijiquan. My primary purpose in writing this book is to inspire all practitioners of Taijiquan (regardless of their level of achievement in the internal arts) to learn and put into practice the Qigong methods presented in this book to help them enrich their lives and advance their knowledge of the art of Taijiquan.

The Origin of Taijiquan

The early development of modern Taijiquan1 is attributed to Zheng San-Feng (1247-1440 CE), a neo-Confucian scholar and highly achieved former Shaolin monk who was an expert in Shaolin White Crane and Snake style Gong Fu, Taoist Dao-yin (Chinese Yoga), and the alchemical arts of longevity. Zheng San-Feng (Figure 1) was alleged to have lived over 300 years. He is credited with founding the Taoist Temple at Mount Hua in the Wu Tang Mountains. Soon after leaving the Shaolin Temple, while resting under the shade of a tree by the side of the road, Master Zheng noticed a snake being attacked by a bird. He observed that although the bird was larger and much fiercer it was unable to subdue the snake. The snake's evasive movements eventually allowed an opening for it to strike — killing the bird, thus inspiring his interpretation of the internal martial arts (Neijia). The original Zheng form had seventy-two postures or movements and contained elements of Gong Fu and Dao-yin. The name Taijiquan (**literally "Grand Ultimate Boxing)"** was allegedly coined by Wang Zong Yue one of Zhang San-Feng's senior students.

Figure 1: Zheng San-Feng ("Zheng")

---

[1] Modern Taijiquan in this context refers to the styles of Taijiquan that we would recognize today.

At one point in his many journeys around China, he arrived at Chen Village (Chen Jia Guo) in Henan Province where he introduced his new style to the aristocratic Chen family. At the time of Zheng's arrival, the Chen family already had a martial art style of their own called "Cannon Fist (Pao Chui)" into which Master Zheng's teachings were later integrated.[2] The Chen style is considered to be the root or 'mother' form of all the modern Taijiquan styles.

Taijiquan (Tai Chi Chuan) is an internal or "soft" style martial art system (Neijia) designed for personal development and self-defense that is based on the principles of the inner-action between yin and yang within the Thirteen Original Postures (Shi San Shi). The Thirteen Original Postures (Figure 2) consist of: The Eight Diagrams (Ba Gua) symbolizing the eight expressions of energy (Jin) used for self-defense applications, The Five Elements (Wu Xing) symbolizing the five stepping patterns (Wu Bu) of the Taijiquan solo form, and Wuji (Wu Chi) symbolizing of the "empty" energy pivot that characterizes Taiji movement and self-defense applications.[3]

The Art of Taijiquan

Taijiquan is practiced world-wide and is an excellent form of movement meditation and exercise that enhances the body, mind, and spirit. There are five popular schools or styles of Taijiquan taught today: Zheng (Chang), Chen, Yang, Wu, and Sun. Yang style is considered to be the most popular because the style embodies what is called "three frames" or three levels of stances and posture

---

[2] It should be noted however that the actual early development of Chen stye Taijiquan is rather vague. The general consensus among modern scholars is that it wasn't until the 9th generation under patriarch Chen Wang-Ting (1550-1660 CE) that the style became well defined.

[3] In this context, pivot refers to the function of the waist that acts like a wheel or fulcrum that can be used to upset or control an opponent's center of balance.

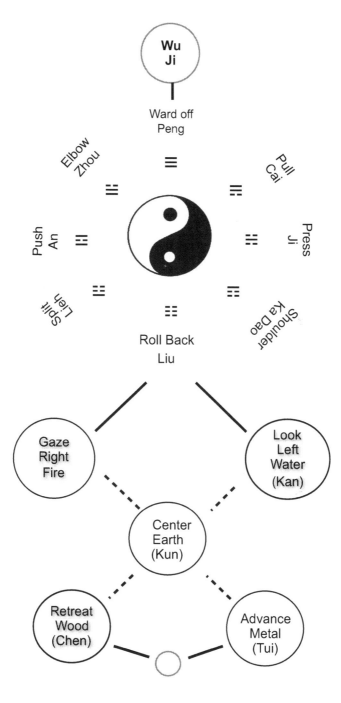

Figure 2: The Thirteen Original Postures of Taijiquan

adjustments: High, Middle, and Low. The Low frame is he most challenging, and requires some degree of athletic ability. The Middle and High frames are the most popular because these styles can be taught to a broader range of people. The High frame postures are better suited to seniors.

Most people begin Taijiquan as a form of gentle aerobic exercise not realizing that it is also a martial art. It should be noted that not all teachers of Taijiquan emphasize its martial art aspect — choosing instead to focus on the gentle movements and breathing techniques of the art to promote its many health benefits.

As a martial art system of self-defense it is one of the most difficult to master as it employs principles and concepts that differ dramatically from the "external or hard style" martial art systems.[4] The hard style systems tend to be better suited for younger people — mainly because of the arduous training regimens involved in mastering the styles. After 20 plus years as a practitioner and instructor of Chinese Gong Fu, I began to experience many of the negative physical effects of practicing the hard style — especially as I began to age. In my opinion, these effects were mainly the result of many years of over-stressing my muscles, tendons, and joints — a common problem for most people. Like many long term practitioners of hard style martial arts I eventually made the decision to revert to a less stressful style so I decided to learn the Yang style of Taijiquan.

It is said that Zheng San-Feng parted with Shaolin Temple because he felt that the Shaolin boxing style and the Qigong[5] methods taught there focused too much on physical muscle-tendon training (Yi Jin Jing) rather than on energy cultivation — basically inferring that Shaolin Temple "taught no longevity."[6]

The internal styles (Taijiquan, Bagua Zhang, Xing Yi Quan and Liu Ho Ba Fa Quan) are considered to be "soft" styles and approach training practically in the

---

[4] Shaolin Kung Fu, Japanese Karate, and Korean Tang Soo Do, or Mui Tai Boxing are considered to be 'hard style schools' of martial arts.

[5] Shaolin emphasized Qigong that trained the body to enhance physical endurance and withstand trauma. Two examples of these methods are Iron Shirt, and Golden Bell Qigong that make the body impervious to blows (not bullets, unfortunately), but have the side effect of seriously shortening a practitioner's life-span.

[6] A quote often used by my Qigong teacher, Dr. Wang Xue Zhi, whose training included teachings by the Taoist Wu Dang master Lan Dan Shu.

5

reverse of the "hard" schools.[7] Internal style schools introduce the students to supplemental energy work (Qigong) from the outset of their training. This internal training is then incorporated into the martial applications and techniques thus building the necessary foundation for systematically increasing potential power (Fa Jin). An In important characteristic of the internal styles (Taijiquan in particular) is that the practitioner trains to always be poised and relaxed — the muscles, tendons and ligaments contain much more intrinsic power when they are relaxed. Another significant difference between the hard and soft schools is that many practitioners of the internal styles remain strong and healthy and continue to practice well into their eighties and sometimes nineties.

From the point of view of an outside observer Taijiquan appears superficially weak compared to the more dynamic looking hard styles. However, Taijiquan at the masters level is very formidable. Externally the body seems as soft as cotton but internally the bones, tendons, and ligaments are strong like steel. Taijiquan is often described by its opponents as *like trying to attack a ball in the water or like trying to subdue a shadow.*[8]

The Principle of Taiji (Tai Chi) in Taijiquan

The original definition for the term "Taiji" comes from the ancient Chinese classic, The Book of Changes (Yi Jing or I Ching), transcribed from ancient Taoist oral teachings sometime during the Zhou Dynasty (H. Ni).[9] An excerpt from in the Yi Jing says: *"..where there is Tai Chi there is peace and harmony between the positive and negative"* (Xingdong 40).

---

[7] Taijiquan is called an internal art because the term "neijia" embodies the principles of learning Taoist inner-alchemy to promote martial power as well as longevity.

[8] In martial applications Taiji acts as an expression of movement that is the result of the neutral pivot (Wuji) between the opposing forces of yin and yang. You can feel this principle if you try to push a ball around in a pool of water. When any pressure is applied, the ball will push back while simultaneously neutralizing the applied force.

[9] The Chinese Zhou Dynasty lasted for over 800 years, and was divided into three periods: The Western Zhou (1045-771 BCE). the Spring and Autumn Period (770-476 BCE). and The Warring States Period (475-221 BCE). The Taoist schools, which were the origin of the philosophy of Taijiquan, arose during the latter two periods. Ni, Hua Ching, translator. I Ching: The Book of Changes and the Unchanging Truth. Sevenstar Communications Group, 1994.

The term Taiji can be thought of as a metaphor for the second phase of creation in Taoist cosmology which states that at the beginning of time there was a state of energy called Wu Chi or Wuji (roughly translated as the state of "non-extremity" or "emptiness"). Symbolically it is represented as an empty circle. However, within the center of this circle there is the infinitely small seed of "creative potential."

According to the Taoist cosmology (Appendix A) the process of creation began the moment some mysterious primordial force intended for movement to begin. As the energy began to manifest and move two opposing forces were created called yin and yang. Because they were opposites they attracted each other and began to rotate forming the energy state of Tai Chi represented by the familiar Tai Chi symbol. When you hear the term Tai Chi, it does not mean exactly the same thing as Taijiquan — rather it refers to the principle of Tai Chi (Taiji) within the martial art system of Taijiquan.

Figure 3: The Taiji Symbol

Health Benefits of Taijiquan

Taijiquan is characterized by flowing movements, which are performed slow while coordinated with the breathing and directed by purposeful mental intent. Combining these three aspects of movement, breathing and mental intent has tremendous health benefits. Moving in the relaxed postures help increase flexibility of the joints and gently strengthens the physical body. The reflexes actually react more efficiently when the muscles are relaxed. The breathing pattern, added to the movements, facilitates the smooth flow of energy (Qi) and circulation of blood while simultaneously acting to massage and stimulate the functions of the internal organs especially the bowel's function of eliminating waste and toxins from the body. Coordinated breathing and movement also stimulates the endocrine and lymphatic systems greatly reinforcing the immune system.

The mind stays focused and calm while performing the Taiji solo form or during meditation. A clear calm mind helps to regulate the emotions which can be a major cause of distress. This is the reason Taijiquan is often called a form of movement meditation. Movement meditation is a form of Qigong — Taijiquan and Qigong share the same roots: they are both based on the same Chinese cosmological principles found in the ancient Chinese text.

According to The Book of Changes (Yijing) the principles of Wuji, Yin and Yang, and the Five Elements along with the Eight Diagrams of the Manifestations of Energy (Ba Gua) can be applied to a broad range of disciplines from philosophy to martial arts, healing practices, commercial businesses, spiritual development, and more.

Chapter 2

Taiji Qigong: The Energetic Foundation of Taijiquan

Taijiquan is built on the foundation of personal energy work called Taiji Qigong that works directly with balancing and enhancing Qi (universal energy), Yi (intent), and Xi (breathing techniques). Over the course of Taijiquan training students learn how to sense and regulate these three important energy aspects.

In order for Taijiquan to be a complete system, Qigong study is essential. My Taiji teacher often told the story about the early training of the famous Taiji master Yang Luchen.[10] As a young man Yang went to work as a servant in the home of the aristocratic Chen family, a clan famous for their martial prowess. The real reason he took on the position of a household servant was to learn the Chen clan's unique martial art style. Since a young age Yang had always had a burning desire to learn martial arts, but finding a competent teacher was extremely difficult — martial training at this time was usually restricted to trusted family members and never taught to outsiders. As a servant going about his daily chores, Yang would lurk in the shadows and watch Master Chen teach his students.[11] After dark, Yang began to train in secret. After a short time, his plot was discovered and Master Chen ordered Yang to spar with some of the students. To Master Chen's surprise, Yang was able to hold his own with his students. Because Master Chen was so impressed with Yang's ability, Yang was allowed to join his class.

---

[10] Yang Lu Chen (Fu Kwei) 1799-1872 CE patriarch of Yang style Taijiquan.

[11] Chen Changxing 1771-1853 CE, 6th generation master of Pao Chui Gong Fu the Chen families version of what became known as Chen style Taijiquan.

As Yang's training continued, he noticed that no matter how much effort and time he put into his practice, the senior students were still far superior in their abilities. So, he decided to do some more spying and find out why. What he discovered was that the senior students were being taught Taiji Qigong. This was the reason the senior students had so much more strength and endurance. Yang realized that he was obviously not being taught the complete Chen style of martial arts. Just as he had done before, Yang began to spy and train in secret, until it became apparent to Master Chen that Yang seemed to know too much. Once again, Master Chen put Yang to the test. Because he had learned much of Chen's secret training, Yang's skill was now very high.

After a few years Yang was granted permission to leave the Chen family and found his own system of teaching with the stipulation that he could not call his style Chen. Yang's style became known as "Cotton Boxing." This story illustrates the importance of adding Taiji Qigong as a supplemental training to regular Taiji practice.

Defining Qigong

Qigong is a product of the Chinese culture, and its roots go back well before the establishment of the first imperial dynasty (about five or six thousand years ago). In Chinese, Qigong is written with two characters. The first character "Qi" is comprised of the ideograms for rice and a cauldron/container below and the ideogram air/vapor/steam/breath/clouds above. The second character "Gong" is comprised of the ideograms for a carpenters square and the ideogram for effort or achievement over a period of time. The term Qigong literally means to learn to put in the work to breathe skillfully.

氣功

Figure 4: Traditional Chinese Characters for Qigong

Most scholars agree that some of the earliest forms of movement Qigong were developed out of ritualistic dancing. The ancient healers noted and documented that the movements of certain dances (particularly those that emulated the movements of certain animals) helped to promote blood and Qi circulation. When some of these exercises were combined with acupuncture and herbal therapies, it was discovered that healing was significantly enhanced (Shih).

It should be understood that exercises like Qigong are not culturally specific to China alone. All the ancient cultures of the world have their own methods of exercising the body, mind, and spirit. Examples include shamanism, yoga, and indigenous people's healing arts.

Qigong by itself should not be thought of as a universal cure-all. Rather Qigong is a form of holistic therapy that invigorates the body, mind and spirit working towards the goal of self-regulation and self-control. When practiced daily Qigong reduces many of the negative effects of the aging process as well as acting as a defense against the invasion of many diseases. For many centuries Chinese medical Qigong has been prescribed by physicians as a supplemental therapy for accentuating the patient's healing process.

Qigong's Divisions and Branches

There are five divisions and two branches of Qigong: Taoist, Buddhist (Religious), Scholarly (Confucian), Medical, and Martial. The five divisions are subsequently divided into two branches: External Elixir (Wei Dan) and Internal Elixir (Nei Dan). The term "elixir" in this context refers to "essence" which

11

"connotes the reality, principle, or true nature of an entity, or its basic property (Pregadio — emphasis mine). " Meaning in basic terms: personal energy cultivation and physical development. Each division or branch has its own objectives: Taoist and Buddhist Qigong focuses on spiritual development. Scholarly Qigong works with increasing intelligence and morale character. Medical Qigong focuses on healing and disease prevention utilizing techniques that balance the physical, energy, and Spirit bodies.[12] Martial Qigong works with methods for enhancing physical strength, endurance, and martial power as well as methods for energy cultivation and longevity.

In regards to the two branches of Wei Dan and Nei Dan training, the first of these branches is called Wei Dan Gong or external elixir work. This branch mainly emphasizes developing the physical aspects of the body — building strength and endurance along with focused mental intent (Yi) and increased resistance to outside influences such as trauma or disease. Wei Dan practice strengthens the body externally by first enhancing the body's Wei-Qi. Wei-Qi or 'Guardian Qi' is the energy that flows in the most superficial layer of the physical body protecting the body against trauma or the invasion of disease. According to Chinese medicine, if a pathogen breaks through the Wei-Qi layer of the body it will invade the superficial (Luo) channels of the body's meridian system and penetrate into the body's interior.[13] The deeper the pathogen penetrates into the interior, the more serious the disease.

Along with enhancing the body's Wei-Qi, Wei Dan supplemental exercises help the practitioner attain better flexibility of the joints and stronger muscles and tendons.

The second branch of Qigong training is called Nei Dan Gong or internal elixir work. The primary focus of Nei Dan training is to increase longevity with the ultimate goal of attaining spiritual enlightenment.

According to the Taoists, the term 'longevity' does not simply mean to live a long time — it really has more to do with the quality of the life you are living. Nei

---

[12] The National Institute for Health recognizes the importance of balancing what scientists call the "Bio-fleld," which is comprised of a bio-electric, bio-magnetic, and spiritual energy independent of our physical bodily functions.

[13] The Luo channels are the most superficial channels of the body's channel system. They are situated in the same area as the Wei-Qi, just under the skin and just above the muscles in an area that covers the whole body called the "Cou Li Space."

Dan Gong eliminates (or at least significantly reduces) the negative effects of aging on our bodies. Because the Taijiquan martial art system embodies a balance of Wei Dan and Nei Dan training methods, many practitioners of Taijiquan are spared the negative effects of aging.

Benefits of Taiji Qigong

How many of us have come home from a stressful day at work only to flop down at the couch totally drained of energy? Our bodies build up tension due to family obligations, lack of exercise, insufficient sleep, poor diet, or exhausting work schedules. Most people's idea of relaxation is to take a vacation, only to come back to start their work-week even more stressed out and exhausted. Where's the relief? If only there was a way to relax. There is. Consider learning Taijiquan and its supplemental energy work Taiji Qigong.

I remember at the beginning of the first Taiji class that I attended: the very first thing the teacher said was: "OK everyone, you can relax your shoulders now." Almost everyone in the class immediately realized that their shoulders were up around their ears. We all subsequently let out a long breath and felt our shoulders soften and relax. This was my first introduction to 'body awareness' where I could actually sense the tension in my body and feel some degree of relief by consciously relaxing when I exhaled.

Taijiquan differs from other styles of martial arts because Taijiquan is performed in a relaxed and emotionally calm state as opposed to styles such as Shaolin Kung Fu, Japanese Karate, or Korean Tae Kwon Do that tend to emphasize building up the muscles to increase martial power — often leading to tense, tight muscles. I studied and taught Hung Gar Kung Fu for more than twenty years. It wasn't until I began Taijiquan and Taiji Qigong training that I learned the importance of relaxation within the movements and postures.

Health Benefits of Taiji Qigong and Taijiquan Practice

- Naturally corrects posture and aligns the body's physical structure increasing range of motion, flexibility, poise and improved balance.
- Exercises all the muscle groups, tendons and ligaments as well as reinforces the skeletal structure.

- Improves the functions of the internal organs and the efficiency of the bowels.
- Aids digestion and nutrient absorption.
- Enhances the endocrine system's ability to ward off illnesses.
- Increases mental focus and acuity.
- Develops 'body awareness' — that is being able to sense your physical body on a subtle energetic level,
- Relieves stress and emotional instability.
- Clears obstructions from the meridian system facilitating the smooth circulation of Qi.
- Assists in detoxifying the five fundamental substances within the body: Shen (guiding spirit), Jing (sexual and vital essence), Qi (natural energy), Jin ye (vital fluids), and Blood (Xue).
- Improves self-esteem and personal confidence.

Chapter 3

Basic Qigong Theory

Now that you have a general understanding of what Taiji Qigong is and what it can accomplish, the following sections will explain the basics of Taiji energy work. The theories presented here will provide you (the practitioner) with the necessary information to ensure a safe and successful practice.

Yin and Yang

The forces of yin and yang first appeared in our universe when some primordial 'will' created a rotation of movement within the 'seed of potential' within Wuji thus creating the two polarities of Qi. Yin-yang polarities are always in flux, whether within the cosmos (macrocosm) or within the human body (microcosm). It should also be noted that the terms of yin and yang should not be given any religious or moral connotations — they are not indicative of either 'good' or 'evil.'

The primary goal of Taiji Qigong training is to develop the ability to recognize any imbalances of the yin and yang energies in our bodies and learn how to restore them to a healthy balance. The most relevant characteristics of the various manifestations of yin and yang are listed in Table 1.

Yang

Yin

Clear, Bright, Hot	Shady, Dark, Cold
Dryness, Fire, Red	Moisture, Water, Black
Day, Upper, Outer	Night, Lower, Inner
Front, Open, South	Back, Closed, North
Straight, Angular	Curved, Spherical
South of the Mountain	North of the Mountain
North of the River	South of the River
Male, Positive, Forceful	Female, Negative, Passive
Cosmological Principle Sun	Cosmological Principle Moon
Spring-Summer	Autumn-Fall

Table 1: Characteristics of Yin and Yang

Five Element (Wu Xing) Theory Applied to Taiji Qigong

Along with the principles of Wu Ji, Yin and Yang, and the Eight Gates, the Five Elements (Figure 5) play an important role in Taijiquan and Taiji Qigong study. In Taijiquan the Five Elements (Table 2) represent the characteristics of certain animals as well as certain techniques used in martial applications. Their use in Taiji Qigong practice is particularly important in regards to the interaction of the internal organs and their associated energy channels combined with the external manifestations of energy of the cardinal directions, our emotions and the seasonal cycles.

According to the Chinese classic the Book of Changes (Yijing) Five Element Theory can be applied to the cycles of Heaven (Cosmological), Earth (Natural), and Mankind (TCM or Martial Arts), and energy cultivation. The Five Elements (also called the Five Activities or Phases) represent the various activities or movements of the essential substances that make up the natural world: Wood-Fire-Earth-Metal-Water. The Five Elements are dynamic and interact with each other.

There are three different cycles of interaction that the Five Elements follow: The Cycle of Generating and Control, the cycle of Over-acting, and the Insulting sequence. The Over-acting and Insulting sequences relate more to their use in TCM mainly as a diagnostic tool and their role in herbal treatments.

For students of Taiji Qigong the cycle of Creation and Control is the one of particular importance. In Figure 5, the sequence of Creation, and Generation is indicated by the dark arrow, and the Control or Destruction sequence is indicated by the gray arrows.

General Characteristics of the Five Elements

- Wood is characterized as a sprouting and spreading activity — like a seed spouting from the earth and developing into a plant or tree.
- Burning Wood creates Fire. Fire is characterized as a yang activity that produces heat with a tendency to flare upward. Fire's burning activity produces ash (Earth).
- Earth is characterized as a neutral activity that is supporting, nourishing, and subject to change. Earth produces minerals (Metal).
- Metal is characterized as a strongly active upward-outward movement with the tendency to expand. The ancient sages observed moisture condensing on Metal and viewed this process as Metal producing Water.
- Water is characterized as a yin activity producing cold moisture and the tendency for downward movement. Water is essential for Wood to grow.

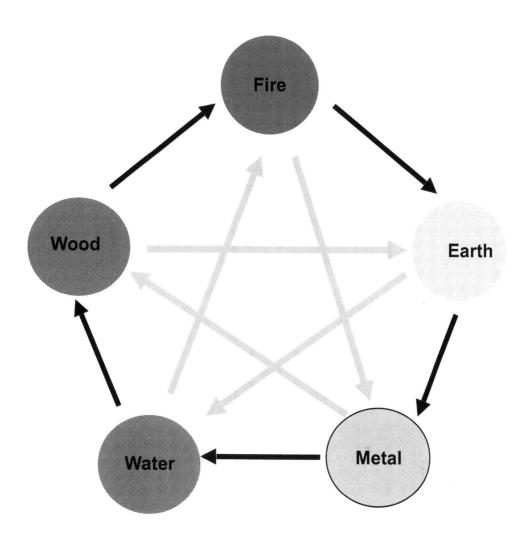

Figure 5: The Five Element Cycles of Generation and Control

Element	Wood	Fire	Earth	Metal	Water
Direction	East	South	Center	West	North
Season	Spring	Summer	Indian Summer	Autumn	Winter
Climate	Wind	Summer Heat	Dampness	Dryness	Cold
Process	Birth	Growth	Transformation	Harvest	Storage
Planet	Jupiter	Mars	Saturn	Venus	Mercury
Animal	Fish	Birds	Humans	Mammals	Shellfish
Domestic	Sheep	Fowl	Ox	Dog	Pig
Grain	Wheat	Beans	Rice	Hemp	Millet
Color	Green	Red	Yellow	White	Black
Taste	Sour	Bitter	Sweet	Pungent	Salty
Scent	Goatish	Burning	Fragrant	Rank	Rotten
Zang Organ	Liver	Heart	Spleen	Lung	Kidneys
Fu Organ	Gall Bladder	Small Intestine	Stomach	Large Intestine	Bladder
Opening	Eyes	Tongue	Mouth	Nose	Ears
Tissue	Sinews	Blood Vessels	Muscles	Skin/Hair	Bones
Emotion	Anger	Happiness	Pensiveness	Sadness	Fear
Sound	Shout	Laughter	Song	Weeping	Groan

Table 2: Five Element Table

19

The Five Elements in Traditional Chinese Medicine (TCM)

The Five Organs (Zangfu) interact and support each other. The Liver (Wood) is the mother of the Heart (Fire). The Liver's function is to store blood, and blood houses the mind — if the Liver is weak, the Heart will suffer. The Heart is the mother of the Spleen (Earth) assisting the Spleen's transportation function. The Spleen is the mother of the Lungs (Metal). The Spleen provides nourishment from food (Ying-Qi) to the Lungs where it interacts with the air to form Gathering (Kong)-Qi. Deficiencies in both Lung and Spleen Qi are common. Lungs are the mother of the Kidneys (Water). Lung Qi descends to meet Kidney Qi, also sending fluids down to the Kidneys. The Kidneys are the mother of the Liver. Kidney yin nourishes the Liver blood. Kidneys control the bones, and the Liver controls the sinews. The bones and sinews are inseparable.

Chinese Medicine uses the principles of the Five Elements as a diagnostic tool for recognizing certain general medical conditions and then planning a course of treatment which may include using massage, acupuncture, moxibustion, or various herbal formulas to increase deficiencies or reduce excesses in the Zangfu and their associated channels. The Five Element's correlation with colors is frequently used as a diagnostic tool in TCM. Doctors observe any unusual colors of the skin, bodily fluids, eyes, or tongue to help determine a treatment strategy for the patient.

The Five Primary Substances and
the Three Treasures (San Bao)

There are five substances in the human body that our health and vitality depend on: Jing, Qi, Shen, Zhi (will power) and Yi (mental intent). The conversion of Jing to Qi, and then ultimately to Shen, is the goal of Qigong training. Jing, Qi and Shen are considered to be the three most vital substances (hence the term Three Treasures) within our bodies that all the other alchemical processes of the human body depend on to function.

Jing

The refinement of Jing (Essence) is the first step in successful Qigong training. Jing is stored and refined in the Kidneys, so maintaining good Kidney health is essential. Qigong training teaches us to conserve our 'Original Essence or Water-Qi.' Water-Qi combines with Fire Essence (Hou-Qi) that comes from the food we eat and the air we breathe. According to Chinese medicine there are two pairs of of organs in our body called Kidneys — the actual Kidneys called the 'internal kidneys' (Nei Shen) and the testicles or ovaries which are called the 'external Kidneys' (Wei Shen). After birth, the Original Essence resides in the Nei Shen. When the Water-Qi is converted to Original (Yuan) Qi, part is used to nourish the external Kidneys and activate the sexual essence (Tian Gui) or hormones. Another part accumulates in the lower Dantien for storage. If the Internal Kidneys are weak and the Original Qi cannot be converted efficiently from the Original Jing, the production of the hormones and Jing from the testicles and ovaries will also be reduced.

Qi

Qi (Chi) is the subtle natural energy that makes up all matter in our universe — from minerals to organic life. According to the Taoists Qi is one energy that has many manifestations. Each manifestation is only a different vibration or frequency of the same energy. For example our blood is considered to be a dense form of Qi. Qi can also refer to breath.

Living beings possess a particularly strong intrinsic energy field that moves around and through them. When this field is disrupted or becomes unbalanced, the result is disharmony manifesting as an illness. If the energy stops completely it means death.

In human beings Qi is has two primary sources — Original (Yuan-Qi) and Acquired Qi.

Original Qi (also called Pre-Heaven or Pre-Natal Qi) is the Qi that we are born with and is derived from the genetic background of our parents and ancestors. Original Qi determines our over-all constitution and health destiny.

Acquired Qi (also known as Post or After-Heaven Qi) is derived from breathing air (Kong-Qi) and the food we eat and drink during our lifetimes. The Qi derived from food is called Ying-Qi. Human vitality (one's overall constitution) depends on the strength of our Upright Qi (Zheng Qi),[14] Congenital Qi (Yuan Qi), and Qi of the internal organs (Zangfu-Qi).[15]

A person's Qi can be affected by the weather, the seasons, good or poor nutrition, electromagnetic fields, or mental attitude (moods or thoughts). Qi is considered to be transcendent which means it can be transferred from one object to another regardless of distance or time. In other words Qi is not bound by the laws of western science. (see Appendix B for Flow Chart of the Source of Qi).

Although Qi is subtle, its effects can be felt — usually as a comfortable warmth or slight tingling sensation during meditation or Qigong practice. The effects of Qi that can be felt are simply an indication of the presence of Qi, not actually Qi itself. Qi has the natural ability to self-regulate itself. However it is wise to pay close attention to those activities in your lifestyle and training that can adversely affect the smooth circulation of Qi within the channels and collaterals of the body.

Qi must circulate smoothly and strongly or it becomes blocked or diverted causing stagnation and exhaustion eventually leading to health problems. This sense of energy within the body is learned from continuous Qigong practice. Qigong methods should be learned step by step. Students should not attempt the advanced levels of practice without first building the proper energetic foundation, because the human body requires time to adapt to the increased energies layer by layer. (Refer to Origin of Qi in Human Physiology Diagram, Appendix B).

Shen

Shen is the Chinese general term for spirit. In the context of Chinese Medicine, Taoist cultivation practices, and the Martial Arts, Shen can be thought of as 'our over-all guiding spirit' that manifests in our personalities or our underlying personal nature. The Shen is said to reside in the Heart. In spiritual terms, Shen is like an Emperor who rules over the spiritual ministers of the other four Zang organs (Lungs, Kidneys, Liver, and Spleen), which seems logical because every

---

[14] The term 'Upright (Zheng)-Qi' is not a specific type of Qi, rather it is a term that refers to the various Qi's of the body working together: Wei-Qi (Guardian-Qi) that protects the body from pathogenic invasion and Ying-Qi which is an internal Qi from which Blood and Jin Ye (vital fluids) are derived.

[15] Zhangfu is the Chinese term for the 5 yin and 6 yang internal organs. Each organ has its own characteristic Qi that mutually interacts with the other organs.

organ of the body depends on the condition of the Heart in order to function. According to Chinese healing arts the mind actually resides in our Heart and not in our brain — so any disturbance of the Shen can lead to many psychological and emotional problems.

Functions of the Three Dantiens (San Jiao)

A basic understanding of the Triple Warmer system is important to Qigong and Taijiquan training because it is a part of our overall energy system that makes our body function. In Chinese Qigong energy cultivation and martial arts, the term Dantien literally means 'elixir or cinnabar field.' The human body actually has three Dantiens which are part of a larger system known as the Triple Warmer, Heater, or Burner (San Jiao in Chinese).

There are four aspects of the Triple Warmer system to consider. First, the Triple Warmer can simply refer to the three divisions of the body (upper, middle and lower). Second, it can also refer to the three large cavities of the body (Jiao) that act as containers or vessels for the Zangfu. Third, the Triple Warmer has its own associated energy channel, and fourth, it works with an additional vessel of the body called the Cou Li Space — the space between the skin and the muscles all around the body.

Each of the three elixir fields has its own function: According to Chinese medical theory, the Upper (Shang Jiao) Dantien is located from the diaphragm upwards to the head and includes the Lungs, and Heart. This is corroborated by the Ling Shu Chapter 30, which states that the *Upper Warmer opens outward and spreads the five flavors of the food essences. It pervades the skin, fills the body, moistens the skin, and is like a mist* (Jing-Nuan 126 — emphasis mine).

The Middle Warmer (Zhong Jiao) is located between the diaphragm and the umbilicus. The Middle Warmer is compared to a maceration chamber or bubbling cauldron. As stated in the Ling Shu Chapter 18: *the Middle Warmer is situated in the Stomach...it receives Qi, expels the waste, steams the Jin Ye (vital fluids)... it refines the essences of food, and connects upwardly to the Lungs.*

The Lower Warmer (Xia Jiao) is like a drainage ditch. The Ling Shu Chapter 18 goes on to say that *food and drink first enter the Stomach, the waste products go to the Large Intestine in the Lower Warmer and oozes downwards, secretes the fluids, and transfers them to the Urinary Bladder* (Jing-Nuan 92-93 — emphasis mine).

The Cou Li Space plays a prominent role in our general health, because this is the area where the Wei Qi circulates and protects the body from trauma and the invasion of disease. Practicing Taiji Qigong greatly fortifies the Cou Li Space.

Because the Triple Warmer is associated with water metabolism in the body, its channel is mainly used in TCM for reducing fevers in the treatment of febrile diseases. In the self-defense aspect of Taijiquan some of the acu-points of the Triple Warmer channel can be used as pressure-points which can inflict pain or paralysis in an adversary.

Functions of the Triple Warmer

- Mobilizes Yuan-Qi.
- Regulates transportation and penetration of Qi.
- Controls water passages, and the excretion of fluids.

Mobilizing the Yuan Qi

Yuan-Qi represents Jing in action in the form of Qi. Yuan-Qi resides between the Kidneys and is closely related to the "Fire of the Gate of Life (Ming Men)." This process is explained in The Classic of Difficulties, Chapter 66 which states: *Below the umbilicus, between the Kidneys there is a motive force (*Dong-Qi*), that is life-giving and the root of the twelve channels (Qi Jie); it is called Yuan-Qi. The Triple Warmer assists the Yuan-Qi to separate into its various functions, such as Qi for use in the internal organs, digestion, procreation, etc.) and controls movement and passage of the Three Qi through the Five Yin and Six Yang organs* (Maciocia 847-848).

Regulating Transportation and Penetration of Qi

- In the Upper Warmer, the Lungs receive Qi in the form of Gathered (Zong)-Qi — a combination of Kong-Qi (air) and Gu-Qi (food essence). This combination produces True (Zeng)-Qi — a purer form of Qi, that then circulates in the organs and channels of the body. True (Feng)-Qi is a combination of Ying (Nutritive) and Wei (Guardian)-Qi that is further refined into Spirit (Shen).

- The Middle Warmer functions as the body's processing plant in which the Stomach receives and the Spleen refines Gu-Qi (food essence) into True (Zeng)-Qi that can be used by the internal organs and vital fluids (Jin Ye).[16] Qi acquired by the ingestion of food and air after birth is referred to as Post-Heaven Qi (Hou Tian Qi). The Spleen is considered to be the 'Root of Post-Heaven-Qi.'
- The Lower Warmer functions as a storage receptacle for both Yuan-Qi also called Pre- Heaven-Qi (Xian Tian Zhi Qi) and Includes the Large and Small Intestines and the Bladder.
- The Chong Mei (thrusting or penetrating channel) should be included as part of the Lower Warmer, because it supports the San Jiao and is the primary vessel for transporting the three substances — Jing, Qi, Shen once they are refined to True (Zeng)-Qi within the San Jiao. The Chong Mai is also associated with menstruation.

Controlling the Water Passages and the Excretion of Fluids

The Triple Warmer (San Jiao) system plays a crucial role in controlling the water passages within the internal organs (Zangfu) in their associated channels (stomach, spleen, kidneys, lungs, large and small intestines) which all have to do with water metabolism. The Triple Warmer also controls the entering and exiting of Qi in the connecting tissues of the body (membranes, collagen, fatty tissue) that surround and support the Zangfu. This function has a powerful effect on the endocrine/immune system.

---

[16] Fluids are called Jin, and are characterized as clear, light, and watery. Jin is yin in nature, and circulates with the Wei-Qi between the exterior of the body and the Cou Li space (area between the skin and muscles). Jin moves rather quickly, and is under the control of the Lungs, which spreads the Jin to the skin all over the body, as well as the Upper Warmer which controls the transformation and movement towards the skin where it performs a moistening function. Jin also has a thinning effect on blood to prevent stasis. Jin is exuded as sweat, tears, saliva, and mucus.

Liquids are called Ye and are yang in nature. Ye are more turbid, heavy, and dense, and circulate rather slowly with the Ying-Qi in the interior of the body. Ye is under the control of the Spleen and Kidneys for transportation, and the Middle and Lower Warmers for movement and excretion. Ye function to moisten the joints, spine, marrow, and brain. Ye also lubricates the orifices of the sense organs (eyes, ears, nose, and mouth).

One of the most important of the internal organs that assist in regulating water metabolism are the kidneys. The kidneys control our innate constitution and are the foundation of the body's vital energy (Dong Qi). The function of the kidneys is to store essence (Jing), control bone growth, produce marrow, control reproduction, and assist in regulating the water metabolism of the body.

The kidneys differ from the other Zang because they are the foundation for all yin and yang energy of the body. They are the origin of the Fire (Li) and Water (Kan) of the body. According to Wu Xing theory the kidneys belong to the Water Element but are also the source of Fire. The kidneys are the 'Gate' that opens and closes in order to regulate the vital fluids (Jin Ye) in the Lower Warmer.

If the 'Gate' is too open (possibly caused by a deficiency of Kidney-Yang), urination will be profuse and urine pale in color. If the 'Gate' is too closed (potentially caused by a Kidney-Yin deficiency), the urine will be scanty and dark. Energetically the kidneys belong to the Lower Warmer and provide Qi to the Bladder to store and and transform urine. The Large and Small Intestines also play a role in separating the pure from turbid fluids which are under the influence of Kidney-Yang. Kidneys receive fluids from the lungs, some excreted, some vaporized and returned to the Lungs to keep the lungs moist. Kidney-Yang provides the heat to assist this function. The kidneys and lungs work together: the lungs have a descending action, and the kidneys respond by 'holding down' Qi. If they fail to do so, the Qi will rebel upwards creating congestion and asthma. Kidneys open in the ears — when weak, hearing may become impaired with possible tinnitus.

The Driving Force of the Lower (Xia) Dantien

The ancients called the Lower (Xia) Dantien *the meeting place of the Five Qi — the source of generating Qi and the root of life.* The Lower Dantien acts as a pivot for transferring and storing Qi of the internal organs (Zangfu) and for promoting the circulation of the various manifestations of Qi throughout the channels and collaterals of the body.

Qi naturally flows through the channels throughout the course of our daily lives. We do not have to use mental intention to decide the direction the Qi flows, as this takes place on a purely automatic and subconscious level. How we breathe can affect the pressure in the lower abdominal cavity. In Qigong, this degree of pressure is controlled with intentional breathing which keeps the lower Dantien gently rotating, completing one complete rotation in 24 hours. (See Chapter 5, Lower Dantien Breathing Instruction). The direction of the rotation is dictated by the Dai Mai (Belt Meridian) implying that the rotation is a horizontal rather than vertical one. The rotation of the Lower Dantien serves as a catalyst for the movement of Qi through the channels, which smoothly circulates around the energy body. See flow chart, Figure 6.

The various circulations of Qi within the body are called "the small waterwheels." The Lower Dantien is considered to be the actual 'waterwheel' that runs the Qi circulating system. In Qigong practice we work towards improving the efficiency of the Dantien by manually taking control of its rotation for a short period of time. Once we have improved its effectiveness, we will then return control of the Lower Dantien to the subconscious where it will continue to run under the control of our breathing.

Now that the reader has a general understanding of the basic energies, and internal processes that Taiji Qigong training works to perfect, let's get into the fundamental methods of how to apply these principles to actual practice.

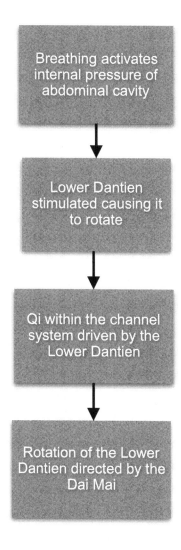

Figure 6: Breathing Activates the Lower Dantien

Chapter 4

Fundamentals of Taiji Qigong Practice

The Three Methods of Preparation for Qigong Practice

Qigong training works with three methods that assist in regulating the smooth flow of Qi throughout the body: Regulating the body, Regulating the Heart/Mind, and Regulating the breath.

1. *Regulating the Body (Tiao Xing)*

Your Qigong practice will be much more effective, if you can learn to relax and release any muscle tension you feel during the course of your practice. The Qigong term for relaxing is "Fa Sung," literally to "sink," which means to be able to relax the body's muscles while simultaneously maintaining a structured posture. When the body is tense, the Qi flow is restricted obstructing and damaging the Qi. Muscle tension can be controlled by using the Yi (mental awareness) to consciously relax the tense areas of the body.

All the varieties of Qigong employ the same five basic postures: walking, standing, sitting, reclining, and kneeling. Each posture has a different function variously affecting muscular tension, the distribution of weight on the different regions of the body, and circulation of Qi and blood. Posture can also affect the function of the internal organs and their corresponding meridians. Whichever posture a practitioner employs, a steady relationship to gravity during practice must be maintained. The body must be as natural, comfortable, correctly aligned, and as relaxed as possible.[17] The necessary requirements for regulating the body are as follows:

- Keep the mind empty and quiet
- Keep the head erect; properly aligned
- Eyes may be slightly open or closed depending on the particular Qigong exercise
- Align the nose with the navel
- Maintain a straight upright spine (avoid slouching)
- Keep the chin lightly tucked inwards towards the neck
- The tongue lightly touches the upper pallet (i.e. the position of the tongue on the upper pallet, when you pronounce the "L" sound in the word "allow")
- Relax the shoulders and elbows
- Keep the armpits open and loose
- Tilt the pelvis back and feel the lower back open around the Ming Men.
- Relax the lumbar and hips.
- In standing postures, keep the knees slightly bent and the feet parallel with the knees.
- If seated on a chair, or bench: sit on the edge of the chair with the genitals suspended; knees align with hips, both feet should be flat on the floor, and aligned with the knees. The chair/bench method works well for beginners.
- If seated on a cushion, use a lotus or half-lotus posture. The cushion method requires more physical endurance which could be difficult for seniors, or people with disabilities.
- The anus should be lightly contracted during practice.

---

[17] The selection of an appropriate posture or position is made on the basis of the characteristics of an individual's body, the disorder or disease being treated, and the duration of the exercise. Postures should not be thought of as static, or rigid; there is some degree of freedom to move depending on the practitioner's disorder, or physical constitution. Practitioner's can make subtle adjustments as the practice or exercise progresses. However, it is not good to change positions too frequently, i.e. fidget around.

2. Regulating the Heart/ Mind (Tiao Xin)

Qigong exercises that concern 'attention' are considered to be exercises for the regulation of the Xin.[18] Attention, in this case, means the experience of both consciousness and the mental activity of the brain. Regulating attention allows the practitioner to further eliminate tension and bring the body into a more receptive, comfortable condition to calm the emotions and eliminate excess mental activity. Studies have shown that eliminating distracting thoughts and inducing a state of mental emptiness and calm through controlled attention and thought inhibits the acquired mind[19] and preserves the Primordial (Yuan) Qi. In our modern society it is practically impossible to be totally free of worry and negative influences. The ancient Chinese physicians and healers accumulated a lot of experience and developed many useful methods in regards to sustaining an easy, calm, carefree lifestyle. The following are some of the most useful examples used by practitioners to control distracting or disturbing thoughts and emotions:

- Reflect on a beautiful scene in nature such as beautiful mountains and rivers, vast seas, flourishing greenery, the silence of morning, or sublime moonlight. Imagine walking through a forest under the canopy of shade trees, or listening to beautiful music. Recall happy events during your life, or think of yourself as youthful, heathy, and beautiful. Listen to the song of birds or insects, the sound of flowing mountain streams or ocean surf.

- Our imagination or visualization can be used to correct unbalanced thoughts and feelings caused by the effects of changes in the seasons or extreme weather conditions. We can manage our internal conditions, such as unpleasant summer heat by imagining a pine tree as it is in winter covered in ice and snow. During the transition of winter into spring, we can imagine the ice and snow of winter beginning to melt and nature awakening. In winter think of the comfortable warmth of summer. Think of water and cold to eliminate heat in the dock, and we may think of fire to remove a chill.

---

[18] The Heart/Mind (Xin) is the Chinese term for the 'mind' or the Heart center, as opposed to the western concept of the mind residing in the brain. According to the Chinese masters, an out of control Xin "is like a monkey running around in a cage," i.e. our thoughts, and imagination running around in our minds incessantly.

[19] The Acquired Mind is basically our egos made up of all the baggage of life.

- Inner quiet may be induced by applying conscious relaxation from the head top down to the soles of your feet, thereby removing distracting, or disturbing thoughts.
- Count your breaths, listen to the sound of breathing thinking *quiet* on the inhalations and *relax* on the exhalations.
- In regards to the specific points of the body, avoid focusing your intent (Yi) too strongly on these specific points. Rather think and feel the energy moving along the corresponding channels 'through' the points instead of directly into them. For example on the inhalation lead the Qi towards the point. On the exhalation direct the Qi through the point. Focusing your attention directly into the acu-points can cause energy stagnation or 'stuck' Qi.

3. *Regulating Respiration (Tiao Xi)*

Breathing is the central aspect of life and the foundation of Qigong practice. The inhalation of breath is considered to be yin and the exhalation an expression of yang. Respiration is literally inhaling the fresh O_2 and exhaling the stale CO_2. Health is profoundly affected by how we breathe. This is why physicians of Chinese Medicine (Zhong Yao) pay close attention to how a patient breathes. The beginning level of Qigong training uses two types of breathing methods: abdominal breathing and natural breathing.

Natural breathing is simply breathing in a relaxed calm manner with no special visualizations. Breathing is spontaneous. The air may or may not be directed to the lower abdomen. This method is usually employed as a preparation for the more active abdominal breathing.

Abdominal breathing promotes the intake of more O_2 and the smooth flow of Qi and blood (Xue) thereby preventing obstruction and increasing the volume of blood flow to the brain and vital organs. Air and food are the 'nutritive' aspects of Qi, and the quality and volume of the intake of these two substances determines a practitioner's physical constitution.

On the inhalation the air is directed in to the lower abdomen which expands outward and on the exhalation contracts inward towards the spine. Breathing should be long, deep, soft and seamless with only a very slight pause between the inhalation and exhalation. With practice the breathing becomes so soft it becomes inaudible.

There are four categories of breathing to consider in Qigong training:

- Feng (Wind) Breathing: breathing that is audible. In most cases this is the starting point for beginners. As your experience increases your breathing should gradually become quieter and quieter. If Feng breathing is not adjusted, you may build up too much Yang-Qi leading to unpleasant effects such as breaking a sweat or becoming mentally agitated.
- Chuan (Asthmatic) breathing: sounds like wheezing and means the exchanges of gases (O_2, CO_2) are incomplete. This leads to energy stagnation and exhaustion.
- Qi breathing: breath is quiet but still audible and not as "threadlike" as it should be.
- Xi breathing: the breathing is exactly correct — without sound or stagnation.

Modern scientific research has confirmed the positive effects of Qigong practice:

- The rate of brain wave activity in the cerebral cortex diminishes, as the alpha wave production increases creating a deep level of calmness.
- Adrenaline increases up to 60% of normal while the secretion of other hormones (such as cortex and growth hormones) decrease. This has a positive effect on the negative effects of aging.
- The rate of protein renewal slows down.
- Enzyme activity changes.
- Cardio-vascular tension is reduced.
- Oxygen consumption is 16% lower than the normal waking state and 6% lower than a state of deep sleep.
- Lactate concentration in the blood is reduced.
- As the diaphragm and abdominal muscles dilate and contract during respiration, gastrointestinal peristalsis is promoted. This in turn promotes the optimal function of the Heart, Lungs, Liver, Spleen, and Urinary Bladder greatly increasing vitality and resistance to disease.
- The whole metabolism of the body slows down. Every cell or tissue decreases consumption and increases their storage of energy potential significantly acting as a preventive factor against disease.

The Wu-Wei Principle: Doing Just Enough

In the initial stages of Qigong practice, breathing with too much force, overdoing movements, and over-visualization can cause several adverse effects. The most common effect is that some people have a hard time going to sleep after evening practices. This could be the result of either putting too much effort into their practice or trying to anticipate effects. This makes the energy too active in the Heart/Mind and increases activity of the brain. In order to resolve this pattern, I recommend practicing lower abdominal breathing, either in a sitting or reclining posture before bedtime to calm things down.

The ancient Taoist masters taught that the best course of action (or non-action) to follow in regards to personal development and energy cultivation practices is to apply the principle of doing just enough with nothing extra called Wu-Wei.

Taoists view the universe as an integral whole — in constant flux. Wu-Wei can be used as a metaphor to guide our conduct and interactions within our daily life. Wu-Wei literally means "not doing" or "without action." However, this does not mean it is best to do nothing. Wu-Wei is the wisdom of doing just enough without unnecessary force, strain, or contention in any situation or endeavor. In doing "nothing extra" one acts spontaneously fully and skillfully out of intuitive wisdom. Another way to look at this is 'not over-doing' or no action out of harmony with natural law.' The spirit of Wu-Wei is demonstrated through the practitioner's commitment to a lifetime of diligent practice and personal development through which the Tao is realized spontaneously and naturally. In Taoism in order to 'not do,' one must first 'do' *"The Tao abides in non-action* (Wu-Wei) *yet nothing is left undone...(*Lao Tzu 39*)."*

Applying the Wu-Wei Principle

Ideally Wu-Wei should not be limited to just Qigong or Taijiquan practice. It should also be integrated into the perfection of whatever art or life path one follows. The martial art of Taijiquan is based on using the soft to conquer the hard, using 'just enough' force or effort in application. Students of Taijiquan learn that being non-confrontational is the correct way to approach any situation: be patient, don't anticipate, react only when necessary utilizing 'just enough' effort.

In regards to practicing Qigong and energy cultivation, I subscribe to the teaching of Lao Tzu and follow the 70% rule. Trying to apply a 100% effort tends to generate too much tension in the body and can lead to potential energy stagnation. The principle of Wu-Wei can apply to cases in which the practitioner is ill, or has sustained an injury. The 'just enough' in this situation refers to how we should approach Qigong practice.

There are two schools of thought on this subject: one school teaches that if you are seriously injured or chronically ill to not practice Qigong until you feel better. Practicing Qigong when you are ill could possibly worsen your condition.

The other school teaches that it is OK to practice, but use only 40 to 50% effort. I subscribe to the latter school of thought. The Taoists believe that the key to healthy living is moderation in all things. 75% of a person's longevity depends on the lifestyle they adopt for themselves.

The Ziran Principle: Go with the Flow

In Taoism, Ziran literally means "self so-doing." It represents the 'spontaneity of naturalness' in human beings. People should attune themselves to the constant transformations of the Tao through cultivation practices such as Qigong or Chinese Yoga (Dao in).

Whereas Wu-Wei represents the (yin) concept of "non-doing" in regards to the natural development of the universe and life, the Ziran principle represents the active, spontaneous (yang) aspect of an unfolding universe which counter-balances Wu-Wei. Wu-Wei and Ziran play prominent roles in regards to our lifestyles: with Wu-Wei we apply just enough effort and with Ziran we go with the flow. The closing lines of verse 25 of the Tao Te Ching (Lao Tzu) admonishes us that following the natural order is the correct path to sustaining vitality and longevity:

....Man follows Earth.
Earth follows Heaven.
Heaven follows Tao.
Tao follows what is natural.

For a stronger energetic connection to nature, I recommend practicing outdoors, whenever the season, or weather conditions permit.

Qigong and the Human Energy Body

The human body is a biological electro-magnetic cellular matrix arranged in layers expanding from the internal to the more subtle external layers. Qi and bio-electricity are synonymous. Our bodies are made up of electrical conductive materials that form an electromagnetic circuit (Yang 46-52).

Bioelectrical energy is produced in the body by the biochemical reaction of food and air which is then circulated around the body by an electromagnet field (EMF) generated by our movements and thoughts. The human body is influenced by natural external electromagnetic forces such as the earth's magnetic field, the Sun, and the electrostatic energy of clouds. Artificial sources of EMF (due to modern technology) are of particular concern and should be taken into account especially when we practice Qigong.

Electro-Magnetic Orientation

When a metal bar is placed in a magnetic field its electromagnetic field will align with that field. The higher the quality of the metal in the bar the better its magnetic alignment. The human body aligns with the EMF of the earth in exactly the same way. The earth's magnetic field flows from south to north and our bodies resonate and align with it. In general the human body's magnetic field is opposite of the earth's. For example in the northern hemisphere the head is the South Pole and the North Pole is at the feet.[20] How we orient our bodies when we practice has an effect on how we interact and receive incoming energy.

The two best directions for practice are either facing south or east. When we practice facing south, the earth's EMF aligns with the microcosmic circulation of energy within our bodies. The front of the body is yin and the back of the body is yang. The yin side of the body tends to absorb energy more efficiently than the back and sides. When the season changes to Spring the Sun's energy begins to

---

20 The opposite of a common bar magnet. More research should be done to understand this effect.

over-ride the earth's magnetic field so it is appropriate to practice facing East. This orientation harmonizes the balance between the yin and yang aspects in our body.

Orienting to an Energy Source

When I was a student training with the late Sensi Dave Harris, one of the many unusual things I noticed about his class was that whenever Sensi was speaking or demonstrating a particular technique his senior students would face him with their hands down next to their sides with their palms turned out facing him. I asked why this was so, and was told that it helps us to absorb the essence of what Sensi is explaining to us even though at that time we had no idea what he is talking about. Later, after the information had time to assimilate in our energy field we are able to almost miraculously put the principle he was trying to convey to us into practice. In this situation it really didn't matter which way we were individually oriented to directionally. All that mattered was that we were facing the energetic source of the information. Qigong practice is much more specific in which direction your practices are oriented towards.

The time of day you practice is a factor to take into consideration. During the daytime the Sun's EMF is stronger than the earth's and during the evening the earth's energy predominates. The ideal time for practicing Taiji Qigong is from sun-up to 9AM facing East. After 9AM the Sun's energy starts to become too yang. Evening practice (i.e. after dark) should face South.

Qi Circulation

Qi is transported around the body via a channel system (Jing Mai) every 24 hours (Figure 7) in a specific order, moving from the deeper layers to the superficial layers and then beginning again at the superficial level. The superficial and sub-dermal layers of the skin is where the Wei-Qi flows. Strengthening the Wei-Qi is the main goal of Martial Qigong. The channels are highly conductive energy pathways that have a positive polarity at one end and negative polarity at the other. The 12 regular channels are connected to the internal organs and have yin and yang aspects that are associated with the Five Zang and Six Fu organs. For example, the Liver is the yin aspect of the Wood element and its yang counterpart is the Gall Bladder. TCM physicians use various treatments to adjust Qi flow or

37

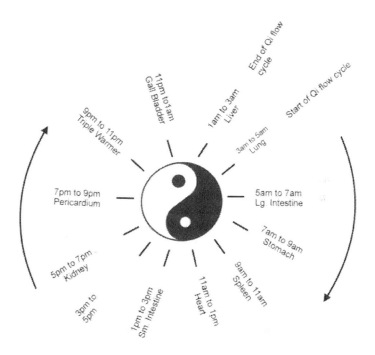

Body Clock
24 Hour Qi Circulation in the Human Body

Figure 7: Body Clock

remove blockages from the channels by applying needles, moxa cones, massage, electricity, or magnets to the slightly more conductive points (cavities or (acu-points) located along these various channels.[21] TCM uses about 2000 of these points to treat patients, as opposed to Qigong and Taijiquan training that usually employ about 36.

Qi Stagnation

Qi can become obstructed in the channels manifesting as stress, pain, urinary problems, abdominal distention, sciatica, joint problems, irritability, depression, or headaches. One theory (out of many) regarding the cause of Qi stagnation is that it is the result of tight muscles and tendons caused by stress. Tight muscles and tendons can cause resistance to the smooth flow of Qi resulting in increasing heat. The sensation of heat in your practice usually indicates some type of blockage of Qi. An ideal sensation would be a slight tingling (like a mild electric current) with little or no feeling of heat.

Practicing the right combination of Qigong exercises on a regular basis will allow the channels to increase their capacity and the increased energy will begin to dissolve away any obstructions. Too little or sporadic practice will not be very effective. Too much practice can make the body too yang — a situation when beginners put too much effort into their practice with the idea that 'more is better.' Whether practicing Wei Dan exercises like Muscle Tendon Changing (Yi Jin Jing) or Nei Dan internal Qi cultivation avoid using too much effort in tensing and releasing the muscles, visualizations, or mental intent. Remember, the mind leads the Qi. Not following this simple rule will agitate the Shen upsetting the spirit and scattering your Qi.

The Five Opening Points — Receiving and Expelling Energy

The Five openings are key cavities located on the channel system from which positive energy is received and negative energy is expelled. The first opening is located at the crown of the head and is called the Hundred Meeting Point (Bai Hui,

---

[21] Applying magnets and electricity to the acu-points is considered controversial to conservative TCM practitioners.

Du-20, refer to Figure 10 later in this chapter). The first pair are located in the feet just behind the ball of each foot and are called the Bubbling Wells (Yong Quan, K-1, Figure 8). The second pair are situated in the center of each palm and are called the Labor Palace Points (Lao Gong, PC-8, Figure 9). These five special points are used to receive healing Qi from the Sun and Moon, earth, nature (plants, trees, animals), the planets, and the stars (mainly the North Star, and the Little and Big Dippers).[22]

The Eight Extraordinary Vessels

The Eight Extraordinary Vessels, or Channels, work in conjunction with the 12 regular channels and the circulatory system to transport Qi and blood to the internal organ systems. Within the regular 12 channels, the yin channels generally flow upwards and the yang channels flow downwards. Contrary to this, within the Qi Jing Ba Mai the yin-yang energies tend to flow in the opposite directions acting to regulate the 12 regular channels and also act as reservoirs that have the ability to absorb and store energy or automatically supply it to the areas of the body where there is a Qi imbalance.

The Eight Extraordinary Vessels are:

1. Du Mai (Governing)
2. Ren Mai (Conception)
3. Dai Mai (Belt)
4. Chong Mai (Penetrating)
5. Yin Wei Mai (Linking)
6. Yang Wei Mai
7. Yin Qiao Mai (Heel)
8. Yang Qiao Mai

---

[22] The ancient Chinese worked mostly with the 5 visible planets (Mars, Venus, Mercury, Jupiter, and Saturn).

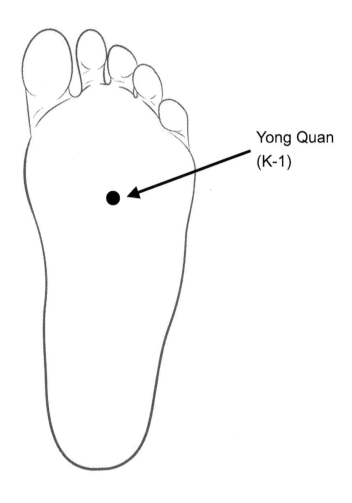

Yong Quan
(K-1)

Figure 8: Yong Quan Point

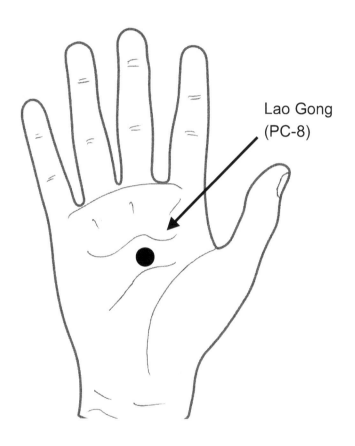

Lao Gong
(PC-8)

Figure 9: Lao Gong Point

The Eight Extraordinary Vessels are considered to be 'extraordinary' because they:

- Do not belong to the main channel system (Jing Mai)
- Do not have interior-exterior relationships
- Add something to the channel system
- Generally flow counter to the regular 12 channels

With the exceptions of the Du and Ren Mai, the Qi Jing Ba Mai do not have their own points as the 12 main channels do, but they do share various points of the main channels.[23] Therefore, each Extraordinary Vessel influences more than one channel which is their important characteristic in both clinical and Qigong practice. Because the Du and Ren Mai have their own points and also act as reservoirs, the number of channels is commonly listed as 14 rather than 12.

Ancient Chinese classical medical literature explains how the Qi Jing Ba Mai function as reservoirs of Qi. The Classic of Difficulties (Nan Jing)[24], Chapter 27, states that *"the sages built ditches and reservoirs, and they kept the waterways open in order to be prepared for above-normal situations [i.e.floods]. When there were heavy rains, the ditches and reservoirs were filled to the brim. In the human body, when the channels are overfilled, they cannot absorb the excess, [and this excess is absorbed by the Qi Jing Ba Mai]"*. Nan Jing, Chapter 28 continues:*"... the overflow is absorbed into the Qi Jing Ba Mai, where they are no longer part of the general circulation."* Li Shi Zhen says, *"when Qi of the channels overflows, it flows into the extraordinary vessels where its turned into irrigation warming the internal organs and irrigating the Cou Li space externally."*[25]

The influence of the Qi Jing Ba Mai on the Cou Li space implies their importance in warding off invading pathogenic factors. The Yin-Yan Qiao Mai (Heel Vessels) are the first line of defense of this function. This is further proof that this pathology consists primarily of excess yin or yang patterns. For example the

---

[23] The Yang Qiao Mai is known by many OMDs as the Yang Heel Vessel. However, the Chinese character 'Qiao' refers to the action of lifting the foot (as in stepping) rather than to just the heel.

[24] The Yellow Emperor's Classic of 81 Difficulties (Ba Shi Yi Nanjing) was compiled during the Han Dynasty. Commonly known as the Classic of Difficulties.

[25] Excerpt from An Exposition on the Eight Extraordinary Vessels (Qi Jing Ba Mai Kao) by Li Shi Zhen (1518-1593 CE) Famous Chinese physician, acupuncturist, herbalist, and scientist active during the Ming Dynasty as quoted by Maciocia (868 869).

Yang Qiao Mai connects with many channels starting from the Bladder and connecting to the Gall Bladder, Large and Small Intestines and then connecting with the Ren Mai and Yin Qiao Mai. This means that the Qi Jing Ba Mai has the ability to both absorb energy from the main channels and transfer energy to where it is needed. This function can occur in cases of shock or trauma for example.

Functions of the Qi Jing Ba Mai

1. Du Mai (Governing Vessel): Regulates the six regular yang channels, which meet at Du-14 located on the upper spine between the 4th and 5th cervical vertebrae. Associated with the physiology of the brain, spine, and reproductive organs.
2. Ren Mai (Conception, or Directing Vessel): Regulates the six regular yin channels and is associated with the Liver, Kidneys and Uterus.
3. Chong Mai: Has a regulating effect on all twelve of the regular channels and is associated with menstruation and the physiology of the reproductive organs. Also considered to be an important link between the Kidney and Stomach channels as well as the Conception and Governing channels.
4. Dai Mai (Belt Vessel): The only horizontal vessel in the body separating the body into two halves. It encircles all the other channels in the abdomen and back like a 'belt.' It is closely related to the Liver and Gall Bladder channels. Associated with the physiology of the lumbar region, abdomen, lower limbs, and the female reproductive organs.
5. Yang Wei Mai (Yang Linking Channel): Has a regulating effect on Qi flow in the six regular yang channels: Large Intestine, Stomach, Small Intestine, Bladder, Triple Warmer, and Gall Bladder. Believed to control the 'defensive' energy (Wei-Qi) of the body and the body's ability to ward off external pathogens (diseases) responsible for controlling the body's exterior regions.
6. Yin Wei Mai (Yin Linking Channel): Has a regulating effect on the Qi flow of the six regular yin channels: Lung, Spleen, Heart, Kidneys, Pericardium, and Liver. Believed to control the nourishing energy (Ying-Qi) of the body and regulates the blood and internal organs.
7. Yang Qiao Mai (Yang Heel Channel): Acts as a bridge linking the primary yin and yang channels. It controls physiologic functions involving the ascent of fluids and the decent of Qi, the opening and closing of the eyes, and general

muscular activity. Also associated with the lower leg muscles, and lumbar region.

8. Yin Qiao Mai (Yin Heel Channel or Vessel): Has a similar function to the Yang Qiao Mai with the additional function of regulating energy in the abdomen and genitals.

Qi Jing Ba Mai Opening or Control Points

These primary control or confluence points described below are located along and communicate with the twelve regular channels (meridians) and are used to activate the Eight Extraordinary channels during Dao-in or Qigong practice. These control points are stimulated by certain movements or mentally activated by directed concentration (Yi) to enhance the energy flow in various areas of the body at specific times. For a visual reference, see Qi Jing Ba Mai charts in Figures 10 and 11.

Qi Jing Ba Mai Opening Points

1. Small Intestine SI-3 (Back Stream — Hou Xi): Activates the Du Mai (Governing channel). When a loose fist is made the point is located in the depression at the end of the crease below the base of the middle finger.

2. Lung Lu-7 (Branching Crevice — Lie Que): Activates the Ren Mai (Conception channel). Thumb side of forearm in crevice at the lateral edge of the radius bone, 1.5 units above the wrist crease.

3. Triple Warmer TW-5 (External Gate or Outer Pass — Wei Guan): Activates the Yang Wei Mai (Yang Connecting or Regulating channel). Located two thumb widths away from the crease of the wrist on the outside of the forearm half way between the bones.

4. Pericardium PC-6 (Inner Gate, or Inner Pass — Nei Guan): Activates the Yin Wei Mai (Yin Connecting or Regulating channel). Opposite TW-5, located two thumb widths above the crease of the inner wrist inside the forearm (between the two tendons).

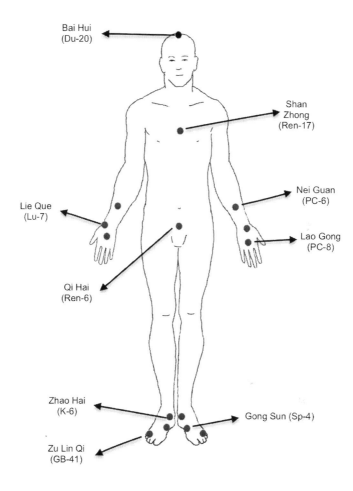

Bai Hui
(Du-20)

Shan
Zhong
(Ren-17)

Nei Guan
(PC-6)

Lie Que
(Lu-7)

Lao Gong
(PC-8)

Qi Hai
(Ren-6)

Zhao Hai
(K-6)

Gong Sun (Sp-4)

Zu Lin Qi
(GB-41)

Figure 10: Basic Control Points Front View

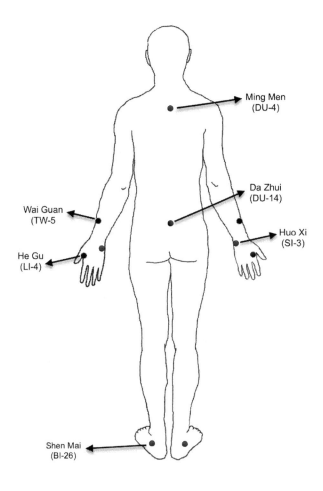

Figure 11: Basic Control Points Back View

5. Spleen Sp-4 (Heredity point — Gong Sun): Activates the Chong Mei (Vitality or Thrusting channel). Located on the inside of the foot above the middle arch in the depression below and in front of the big toe.
6. Gall Bladder GB-41 (Fallen Tear — Zu Lin Qi): Activates the Dai Mai (Belt channel). Approximately one inch toward the ankle from the junction of the two smallest toes (located in the depression behind the small tendon and between the toes).
7. Urinary Bladder Bl-62 (Expanding Vessel — Shen Mai): Activates the Yang Qiao Mai (Yang Heel or Linking channel). Located in the depression just below the tip of the outer ankle bone.
8. Kidney K-6 (Illuminate the Sea — Zhao Hai): Activates the Yin Qiao Mai (Yin Heel or Linking channel). Located opposite B-62 in the depression just below the tip of the inner ankle bone.

Dissolving 'Stuck' Energy

The focus of Qigong practice is to work towards increasing the quality and quantity of Qi and improve its circulation around the body. Energy stagnation could be the result of an injury, poor posture, or various diseases that cause imbalances in the internal organs — the Kidneys or Liver in particular). The Energy Gates is a term used by Qigong and Dao-in practitioners to denote certain areas that lay along the channels where energy could potentially become obstructed or 'stuck.' A common place where obstructed energy occurs is in the joints. Joints are places where Qi and blood gather then enter the interior. When there is extreme stagnation in the joints a condition called Painful Obstruction (Bi) Syndrome develops. Bi Syndrome can be treated by TCM or prevented by continuous Qigong practice. Earlier we said that "Qi behaves like water" — smooth, clear, and flowing — not blasting out like a firehose.

Trying too hard is like trying to flush out the obstructions with a firehose. This can be extremely harmful to the body, because instead of slowly dissolving the obstructions the stagnant energy can be pushed deeper into the tissues and organs. In practice we only want to increase the strength of Qi slightly above normal levels. Too much at once can be damaging to the internal organs. With dedicated daily practice our channels will gradually become larger and Qi levels will increase and begin to eventually clear the channels of obstructions and stagnation. This process takes time. In order to keep things safe, increase your practice duration and the number of exercises step by step. Keep it comfortable. Know your limit.

I have presented you the reader with the basics of Qigong theory — next we can proceed to learning the energy foundation exercises and put these theories into actual practice.

Chapter 5

Basic Standing Meditation (Zhan Zhuang)

Zhan Zhuang (pronounced *"Jan Jong"*) literally translates as "holding the post" and is used as a general term for standing meditation. In Zhan Zhuang training students learn to meditate while standing in various stationary postures while simultaneously concentrating on relaxing the muscles and tendons, releasing pent up tension within the postures, improving breathing techniques, and working with posture alignments that assist the smooth flow of Qi.

There are five levels of training that a student needs to work through to perfect their Zhan Zhuang practice:

- Level One deals with learning to remain relaxed and calm under stress while maintaining the potential for movement.
- Level Two trains the sense of center and improves balance for a firm stance (foundation).
- Level Three involves the collection, maintenance and storage of Qi along with the elimination of toxins.
- Level Four focuses on the elimination of mental clutter (excessive thinking) and visualization techniques to sharpen intent or awareness (Yi).
- Level Five works with specific breathing (Xi) and energy circulation techniques.

The above points should be applied to your practice step by step. Whichever training program you adopt, consistency and the duration of practice are the keys to achieving reasonable progress and ultimately success.

Zhan Zhuang Breathing Methods

Taijiquan students are introduced to the fundamentals of lower abdominal breathing in the basic warm-up exercises and come to understand the importance of correct breathing — coordinating breathing with movement, led by intent (Yi) in their form work. The Taoist classics refer to correct breathing as *"like a silkworm, reeling silk."* The breathing should be as 'seamless' or as 'threadlike' as possible with very slight pauses between the inhalation and exhalation. Stopping and starting the breath during Zhan Zhuang practice may cause energy to stagnate. It is very important that the breathing is never forced.

In Zhan Zhuang practice breathing is usually even (50% inhale-50% exhale) done exclusively through the nose. Movement Qigong often employs nose-mouth breathing, inhaling through the nose with the tongue on the upper pallet and exhaling through the mouth with the tongue neutral.

By contrast when performing or practicing Taijiquan the breathing is 'strategic,' coordinated specifically with the technique or activity of the moment rather than trying to breathe equally.

Lower Dantien Breathing

There are three main methods of lower Dantien (abdominal) breathing employed in Taiji Qigong: Natural, Buddha Breathing and Taoist Breathing. The choice of the breathing method should depend on your level of training and experience. Natural breathing during Qigong practice is distinctly different than simply breathing naturally. In Natural breathing, the breathing is relaxed without any special attention to the movement of the lower abdomen. As the practice progresses, the body becomes more and more relaxed; the mind gradually becomes free of distracting thoughts; entering a calm peaceful state of inner-quiet. *Many schools of Qigong and Taijiquan use this method as an introduction to conscious breathing.*[26]

---

[26] Conscious breathing — breathing in such a manner that the mind is aware of any tension in the body and consciously releases the tension on the exhalation —relaxing deeper and deeper as the practice progresses.

Buddha breathing is the foundation method used in Qigong and in the beginning phase of Taijiquan. The belly moves outward on in inhalation and contracts inward towards the spine on the exhalation. This method increases the O_2 in the lungs which oxygenates the blood and energizes the body. The rhythm of the breathing coupled with the movement of the abdomen massages the internal organs and increases lymph circulation (MacGill).[27]

Taoist or Reverse Breathing is taught after Buddha Breathing is well established. The belly moves inward towards the spine on the inhalation, and expands outward on the exhalation. *Caution: This is an advanced breathing technique that produces much more energy, so it must be developed slowly.*

Basic Zhan Zhuang Preparation

In order for your practice to be safe and effective certain rules should be closely followed:

- Chose an appropriate practice space or area that fits within the requirements of the Six Conditions.
- Chose the appropriate orientation for your practice: facing East during morning hours, or facing South, after sundown.
- As you begin, make sure that you are meeting all of the requirements discussed in Chapter 4 under the Three Methods of Qigong Preparation: Regulating the Body, the Mind, and the Breath.

---

[27] The Lymphatic system has three primary roles: (1) part of the immunological system, (2) maintains the balance of body fluids, (3) lymph is essential for the body's absorption of fats, and various soluble nutrients.

The Six Conditions

The Six Conditions can be applied to climatic conditions, the energetic influence of each season, diet, or the living conditions in your immediate practice area — indoors or outdoors.

1. Hot	4. Dry
2. Cold	5. Wind
3. Wet	6. Fire

- Do not practice in extreme temperatures whether indoors or outdoors. Not too hot or too cold. Keep it comfortable.
- Do not practice in artificial environments, such as air conditioned rooms, freezers, in the proximity of EMF producing appliances — cell towers, transmission lines, active radar, fluorescent lighting, etc.
- Do not practice in damp conditions — rain, fog or on a wet lawn.
- When practicing in arid conditions, practicing in the morning or late evenings is less stressful on the lungs.
- Do not practice in windy or drafty conditions.
- Do not practice directly after consuming a large meal, after engaging in hard physical labor, or directly after sexual activity.

Additional Conditions

- Do not practice Taiji Qigong when you have a cold or flu — especially in group settings. There is the possibility of spreading your contagious pathogens to other people or pushing the disorder deeper into the interior of your body. Wait until you are sufficiently recovered before resuming practice.
- For women, it is generally OK to practice the basic Qigong exercises during the menstrual cycle or when pregnant. In order to be safe, the exercises using lower stances and stronger visualizations should not be performed when pregnant — particularly those meditation methods that use visualizations. Visualizations produce very strong yang energy that could over-stimulate the fetus.
- Following any abdominal surgery, consult your healthcare provider prior to practicing Taiji Qigong.
- Never practice Qigong in an agitated emotional state. If you are upset, try to do some lower abdominal breathing to help calm your emotions down.
- Zhan Zhuang is usually practiced during the day time. Practice in the evening is still OK as long as you don't practice too close to bedtime. Allow at least a couple of hours for the energy to settle down before trying to sleep.

Preparation exercises help to make your body more receptive to acquired energy, and practicing the basic closing exercises (discussed in the next chapter) allows time for your body to assimilate the new energy. When you are practicing any form of Qigong, always pay close attention to how you are feeling: before, during and after practice. Allow your intuition to guide you. Tips on refining your practice will be included in the instruction sections.

Basic Zhan Zhuang Instruction

The following method was initially developed by the Yang Taijiquan family, but keep in mind that it is based on principles that are universal to all styles of Taijiquan.

First Posture—Emptying

1. Begin in a standing posture with feet shoulder width pointed forward in line with the knees, head up with chin lightly tucked inward towards the throat, back straight, knees slightly bent, tongue lightly touching the upper pallet behind the front teeth, and shoulders relaxed with arms hanging relaxed at your sides. (Figure 12. Eyes are either closed or slightly open directed towards the end of your nose or towards a spot on the ground in front of you.

2. Begin breathing into your lower abdomen focusing the air into the Lower Warmer. *Inhale, the belly expands slightly; exhale, the belly slightly contracts inward towards the spine.*

3. Perform six breathing cycles. On each inhalation, try to keep the mind clear of thoughts and expectations. On each exhalation, try to feel the tension of your body draining away (emptying) step by step with each breath. Shifu Andrew Dale taught us the visualization of imagining ice and snow melting off of a mountain and the water (tension) dripping into the earth.

4. Continue to breathe in this pattern for six to 12 cycles.

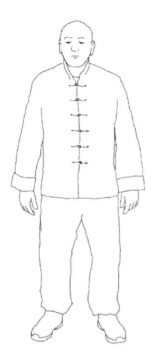

Figure 12: Emptying

Holding the Post:

1. Sit down into a comfortable horse stance (Ma Bo) feet should be slightly wider apart than your shoulders; bring up your arms forming a circle with the hands no higher than your shoulders. Palms are facing inward with the fingers corresponding — thumbs and fingers pointing towards each other (Figure 13). Holding the Post looks something like holding a beachball against your chest. Make sure the elbows stay down, as if they are resting comfortably on a shelf. Knees are bent so that the knees do not extend beyond the ends of your toes. Tuck the tailbone under (you should feel the lower back opening up slightly). Keep your back straight, with the chest relaxed.
2. Inhale. Imagine and feel energy coming from the ground thought the Yang Quan points (K-1) in the soles of your feet up along the inner legs to the Middle Warmer located between the sternum and navel.
3. Exhale. Imagine and feel the energy moving from the Middle Warmer back down into the Lower Warmer (Dantien) located internally behind the navel and approximately one centimeter above the perineum.
4. Repeat Steps 2 and 3 at least 8 to 12 cycles.[28]

Note: Use caution on the length of the breaths (no more than 5-seconds on the inhalation and 5-seconds on the exhalation). Beginners should stay in their comfort zone. Over-doing can possibly make the body too yang with the following symptoms: Increased blood pressure, mental hyper-activity, or deviation of Qi which can potentially harm the internal organs or the nervous system. To be safe increase the length of the breathing cycle slowly over time.

---

[28] A breathing cycle refers to one inhale, followed by one exhale. Never hold your breath; try to keep the breathing as seamless as possible, (almost as if there is no pause) Duration of Zhan Zhuang can vary with experience. Beginners should practice 10 or more breathing cycles per posture, or 5 to 8 minutes. Increase duration gradually.

Figure 13: Holding the Post

Basic Zhan Zhuang Short Closing Exercises

Closing exercises allow additional time for the acquired Qi from your practice to stabilize and become assimilated into the muscles, tissues, and organs. Even though Basic Zhan Zhuang is usually of a shorter duration (approximately 5 to10 minutes) than some of the more advanced standing practices, it is still important to perform some simple closing exercises.

Instruction for Basic Zhan Zhuang Short Closing Exercises

1. Twisting: standing with feet shoulder width turn the waist side to side keeping the arms completely relaxed. Allow your turning waist to move your arms. The palms patting the energy channels of the abdomen (Sp, Lv) and the back of the hands patting the (kidney areas) on the back of your body. *Keep your feet flat on the ground — shifting your weight without lifting your feet.*
2. Turn the Waist and Look Back: Continue twisting as in step 1, alternately looking back over your shoulder. Pat the top of your right shoulder while you turn your to the right. Opposite hand pats the back Kidney area.
3. Turn and Pivot: Continue twisting as in step 2, alternately pivoting on the heel of the empty side. *The gentle tapping on the front and back of your body help to break up any residual stuck energy. The twisting motion of the waist helps stimulate the meridian system.*
4. Bouncing: standing with feet shoulder width, use your thighs and spine to swing your arms up and forward crossing the wrists at about chin level. Arms are completely relaxed.
5. Bouncing Left and Right: Step back into a Left Cat Stance. Use thigh of the grounded leg to push off creating a 'ripple' up your spine that propels the arms forward and upward to about chin level. Perform in sets of 12 on both sides.

Refining Basic Zhan Zhuang Practice

Possibly the most difficult part of standing meditation for beginners is learning self-control. In many cases, overcoming our own egos is the primary obstacle to successful meditation practices. Mastering the breathing techniques and adjusting the postures are relatively easy compared to quieting the mind of internal dialogue, and calming the emotions. In our modern society it is practically impossible to be totally free of worry and negative influences.

If you begin to experience any negative effects, review The Three Methods of Preparation in Chapter 4. Once the practitioner is able to master these fundamentals, he or she will attain a level of 'inner stillness' free from outside distractions and attachments. It is OK to experiment to determine which techniques work best for you:

When there are unbalanced feelings caused by changes in the seasons, weather, or directly regulated to an internal condition (Shih 39), think of water and cold to eliminate heat from the body or think of heat and fire to eliminate chills. For example:

- If you are feeling cold, visualize or imagine that it is a warm pleasant Summer day.
- If you are feeling hot, imagine a snow covered forest or any Wintery scene you can imagine with the snow and ice beginning to melt.
- If you are having trouble concentrating on your practice:
- Try counting the breaths while thinking 'quiet' on the inhalation and 'relax' on the exhalation.
- Listen to the sound of your breathing.
- Use your attention to follow movement of the lower abdomen. Notice the lower abdomen.
- Expand on the inhalation and contract on the exhalation.

As a prerequisite to learning Taiji Qigong, at least a rudimentary knowledge of human anatomy and physiology would be useful — for instance a general understanding of the locations and functions of the components of the human body (the internal organs, for example will help with some of the visualizations and inner--focus in your Qigong training.

Chapter 6

Intermediate Zhan Zhuang

By the intermediate stage in Taijiquan training, students should have enough command of their particular styles solo form that it is practically 'second nature' to them — they are not having any problem remembering the form posture sequence. Once this level is achieved, the next step is to work on 'perfecting' or 'refining' the solo form. At this stage of training much more emphasis is placed on the energetic connections of the postures and transitional movements. In order for a student's energy to develop properly, they need to learn the next level of Zhan Zhuang practice that works on the various energetic aspects of their physical and energy bodies. Yang style Wei Dan Gong is one such method.[29] Instead of standing exclusively in the 'holding the post' posture, Wei Dan Gong works with several postures that each develop their own energetic characteristic. (Refer to the Specific Energy Characteristics of the Yang Dan Gong Postures listed below).

---

[29] I use the Yang Dan method here because it was part of my early training, and I found it very practical.

10-Posture Wei Dan Gong Zhan Zhuang Instruction

Wuji Posture

Begin with Wuji (Empty Vessel) posture as previously explained in Basic Zhan Zhaung practice: Back straight, shoulders relaxed, knees slightly bent. Tongue touches the upper pallet behind the front teeth (*the proper position of the tongue is found by pronouncing the word "allow" or "let" and noticing where the tongue touches the upper pallet of the mouth on the "L" sound*).

Visualize that your spine is a string of pearls suspended from a tree branch, gently swaying in a warm breeze. Keep the head top erect. Systematically, use your awareness to relax your body by feeling the tension and tightness leave the muscles and drain into the ground. Clear the mind of all thoughts, attachments and images. Adjust the breathing (refer to Zhan Zhuang Breathing Methods in Chapter 5). Strive towards softening the breath — so quiet that your breathing is practically inaudible.

Yang Wei Dan Gong Practice Sequence

1. Monkey Holds Cauldron
2. Holding Up Mt. Tai Left
3. Holding the Universal Post
4. Holding Up Mt. Tai Right
5. Pressing Down the Earth
6. Playing the Lute Left
7. Playing the Lute Right
8. Retreat to Ride the Tiger Left
9. Retreat to Ride the Tiger Right
10. Holding the Baskets

Monkey Holds Cauldron

1. Open stance by spreading your feet to approximately shoulder width and dropping into a Horse Stance. Bring your arms from your sides forming a circle with the palms facing the lower abdomen (as if holding a cauldron or ball against your lower abdomen (Figure 14).
2. Inhale: imagine energy coming up from the earth through your Yong Quan (K-1) points in the soles of your feet — up the inner legs to the Middle Warmer.

3. Exhale: imagine and feel the energy moving from the Middle Warmer into the Lower Warmer.
4. Repeat steps 2 and 3, six or more times.

Figure 14: Monkey Holds Cauldron

Holding Up Mt. Tai Left

1. Step out with the Left foot into a Bow Stance raising arms so that the palms are turned up towards the sky (Figure 15).[30]
2. Inhale: image energy coming down from above and entering the palms continuing down to the Middle Warmer.
3. Exhale: feel the energy sinking from the Middle Warmer into the Lower Dantien.
4. Repeat parts 2 and 3 six or more times.

Figure 15: Holding Up Mt. Tai Left

---

[30] Bow Stance, also called a 60/40 stance. Front leg is bowed slightly forward with weight about 60%. The back leg is relatively straight with the knee slightly bent with the weight at about 40%.

64

Holding the Universal Post

1. Step back with your Left foot into a Horse Stance while bringing your arms down to form a circle in front of your chest (Figure 16). *Thumb and fingers should correspond.*
2. Inhale: imagine energy coming up through the soles of your feet, on up along the inner aspect of the legs to the Middle Warmer.
3. Exhale: imagine and feel the energy moving from the Middle Warmer around the inner aspects of the arms returning to the Middle Warmer, then continuing down to the Lower Dantien.
4. Repeat steps 2 and 3 six or more times.

Figure 16: Holding the Universal Post

Holding Up Mt. Tai Right

1. Step out with the Right foot into a Bow Stance raising arms so that both palms are turned up towards the sky (Figure 17).
2. Inhale: image energy coming down from above and entering the palms continuing down to the Middle Warmer.
3. Exhale: feel the energy sinking into the Lower Dantien.
4. Repeat parts 2 and 3 six or more times.

Figure 17: Holding Up Mt. Tai Right

Pressing Down the Earth

1. Step back with your Right foot into a Horse Stance while bringing the arms out with the palms facing down (Figure 18).
2. Inhale: imagine and feel energy coming into the palms and moving back down your arms to the Middle Warmer.
3. Exhale: feel the energy sinking into the Lower Dantien.

Figure 18: Pressing Down the Earth

Playing the Lute Left and Right

1. Step back with your left foot into a Seven Star Stance while raising arms in the Playing the Lute — Left posture (Figure 19A). The Seven Star Stance is similar to a Cat Stance, only the heal rests on the ground and the front toe is raised. Weight distribution is 80% on the back leg and 20% on the forward foot.
2. Inhale: imagine and feel the energy coming down from above into the head top on down to the Middle Dantien.
3. Exhale: send the energy out the ends of your fingers, while simultaneously directing your level gaze to the horizon and into infinity.
4. Switch sides stepping back with your right foot into a Seven Star Stance while raising arms in Playing the Lute — Right posture (Figure 19B). Repeat steps 2 and 3 above.

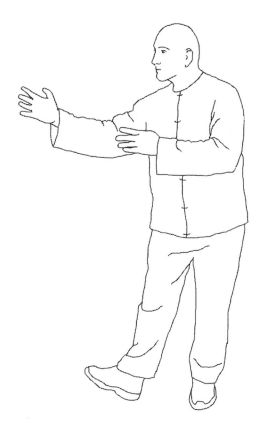

Figure 19A: Playing the Lute —Left

Figure 19B: Playing the Lute — Right

Retreat to Ride the Tiger Left and Right

1. Step back with your left foot into Retreat to Ride the Tiger — Left stance (Figure 20A). For the posture for Retreat to Ride the Tiger stance your weight is 100% on back leg. Your waist and shoulders are turned square to the corner (45°).
2. Inhale — imagine and feel energy coming down through the head top and filling your body.
3. Exhale — Use your Yi (intent) to direct energy back into the earth. *Gaze is directed towards the ground a few feet away from your body.*
4. Repeat parts 2 and 3 six or more times.
5. Switch sides stepping back with your right foot into Retreat to Ride the Tiger — Right stance, again with your weight 100% on the back leg and your waist and shoulders turned to the corner (45°). See (Figure 20B). Repeat steps 2 through 4.

Figure 20A: Retreat to Ride the Tiger — Left

Figure 20B: Retreat to Ride the Tiger — Right

Holding the Baskets

1. Step back into Horse Riding Stance bringing arms out to the sides of your body forming two circles (as if holding two baskets under your arms, (Figure 21). Imagine and feel that the Three Danteans as subtly glowing balls of light. Sense that the Three Dantiens are connected by a vertical column of light that radiates down from above into the head top then passes down through the Three Dantiens and out the perineum into the center of the earth.
2. Inhale — imagine and feel the column of light and the Three Dantiens expand.
3. Exhale: imagine and feel the column of light in the Three Dantiens contract.
4. Repeat breathing sequence six or more times.

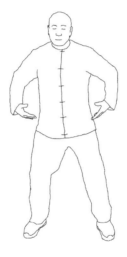

Figure 21: Holding the Baskets

Closing Meditation — Returning the Qi to the Originating Source

1. Bring your hands down and form a Peach Posture (Figure 22), forming a triangle with the thumbs and the index fingers touching (*the thumbs are on the navel*). Gradually return your mind to normal awareness and resume natural breathing.
2. Sense that your body is filled with subtle energy and that you are warm and comfortable. Allow the feeling of peace and well-being continue for as long as you like.

Figure 22: Return to the Source

Intermediate Zhan Zhuang — Closing Exercises

Closing exercises are especially important at the conclusion of a long duration Zhan Zhuang practice of 20 to 30 minutes or more. If you practice only a few minutes you may perform a shorter closing sequence by simply rubbing the palms together and performing a short pat down or beginning your Taijiquan supplemental Movement Qigong exercises.

1. Rub the palms together until hot. Cover your eyes with your palms. Feel the warmth passing through the eyes on through the back of the head into infinity.
2. Massage the face, particularly around the eyes and mouth.
3. Use the tips of your fingers to comb the scalp — front to back, top to sides.
4. Use the index fingers and thumbs to massage the outer rim of the ears from top to bottom, gently tugging on the earlobes.
5. Pat down the front of your body form head to feet. *Patting down helps break up any residual stuck energy.*
6. Pat down both of the arms from the shoulder to the wrists — inside and outside.
7. Beating the Heavenly Drum: cover your ears with your palms and use your index finger to snap over your middle fingers to gently tap the back your head on the occipital lobes 36 times. This creates a resonant 'drumming' sound in your head.
8. Make a loose fist and gently tap the kidney areas. Continue down the back of the legs.
9. Crane Dipping Water: perform a vertical forward circle with your chin to gently loosen the neck.
10. Pushing and Pulling the Qi Ball: harmonizes yin and yang elements in the body. Raise arms into Holding the Post Posture with the palms facing each other. Inhale; feel the ball expand — when you exhale feel the ball contract. Eyes are half-open with the gaze on the finger tips. You may notice light coming out of or around the fingertips.
11. (Optional): Return to Youthful Essence visualization.[31] Bring palms together in front of your Heart. Imagine that you are 14 (female) or 16 (male) years of

---

[31] I learned three different versions of Returning the Qi to the Source. The one presented here is the most basic — the one I include in my personal practice and teachings.

age[32] — in perfect health — full of energy and vitality — surrounded and nurtured by a subtle golden light. Smile inwardly and outwardly, thinking of a happy positive time in your life.

Visualizations for the 10 Wei Dan Gong Postures

1. Monkey Holds Cauldron: Imagine breathing in through the Yong Quan points (Bubbling Well K-1) located just behind the ball of each foot; the energy then continues moving up the inner legs (Leg Yin channels, Sp, K, Lv) to the Middle Dantien. *The ball or cauldron you are holding is actually resting internally on the front of your spine, i.e. think of the ball as three dimensional.*

2. Holding Up Mt. Tai: Imagine that your palms are holding up two balls of light. Feel the connection of Heavenly-Qi descending from above and flowing down through the balls of light into the Middle Dantien.

3. Holding the Universal Post: As you Inhale, imagine and feel the energy flowing up from the Yong Quan points up the inner legs (Leg Yin channels) to the Middle Dantien. As you exhale, imagine and feel the Qi circulating around the insides of your inner arms (the Arm Yin channels and the Yin Wei Mai to the opposing fingers, then returning to the Middle Dantien and down to the lower Dantien.[33] *Energy circulates clockwise for males — counterclockwise for females.*

4. Pressing Down the Earth: Imagine and feel the Earth energy drawn upwards into the Lao Gong (PC-8) points located in the centers of your palms, along the inner arms following the Arm Yin channels and Yin Wei Mai into the Middle Warmer, then directed down into the Lower Dantien.

5. Playing the Lute: Feel the connection between the head top (Bai Hui, Gv-20), the center of the perineum (Hui Yin, Co-1), and the Yong Quan (K-1) point of the weighted foot. This posture works with directing and expanding the Yi (intent or attention).

---

[32] Women's reproductive essence (Tian Guai) awakens at the time they reach puberty at age 14 — men at age 16. The important part of this visualization is to imagine yourself full of youthful vitality.

[33] Yin Wei Mai is one of the eight extraordinary channels that energetically link the top and bottom parts of the body.

6. Retreat to Ride the Tiger: This posture is similar energetically to Playing the Lute. Imagine breathing in through the Bai Hui. Instead of leading the energy exclusively to the Middle Dantien, imagine you are filling your whole body with light. On the exhalation focus the gaze (intent) on a point on the ground or floor a few feet away from your body. Gazing at the fixed point acts as a kind of 'anchor' for your balance while standing on one leg. In my opinion, this posture also works with the Zhi (Will Power), because I have found through practice experience that it takes special concentration to maintain one's center in one legged postures.

7. Holding the Baskets: This posture helps improve the function of the Triple Warmer system (San Jiao) — its channels and body cavities. Stimulating the San Jiao channels benefits the skin, muscles, membranes (Huang), diaphragm and fatty tissue (Gao) of the body. The San Jiao body cavities act like containers for the internal organs and the walls of the vessels act to regulate water metabolism. Visualizing expanding and contracting the central axis that link the San Jiao enhances the endocrine and immune systems. I believe this also strengthens the Chong Mai or Penetrating Channel, one of the eight extraordinary vessels. The Chong Mai has a regulating effect on all twelve of the regular meridians and is associated with menstruation and the physiology of the reproductive organs. It is also considered to be and important link between the Kidney and Stomach meridians, as well as the Ren and Du Mai (Mariocia 868-874).

8. Peach Posture: Hand posture (Shou Jue or Mutra) with thumbs touching at navel and index fingers forming a triangle over the Dantien. (See hand position in Return to the Source.) Return to normal awareness and breathe naturally. Sense that your body is filled with a subtle energy that is warm and comfortable. Allow the feeling of peace and well-being to continue as long as you feel necessary.

9. Return to the Source 3 times.Return to the Source: Step up with feet even, shoulder width. Inhale. As arms move out to your sides to shoulder level with palms facing downward (imagine connecting with the energy of the earth), continue bringing up the arms until the palms are slightly overhead with palms facing towards the sky (connecting with Heaven energy); slight pause in the breathing, then as you exhale bring the arms down with the palms pushing down towards the earth. When you get to waist level bring the palms around

your back by the kidney areas, then back around front to form a Peach Posture (hands form a triangle by touching thumbs at navel, index fingers together (Figure 23).

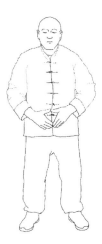

Figure 23: Return to the Source

Refining Wei Dan Gong Zhan Zhuang Practice

Wei Dan Gong practice follows the same rules and conditions previously outlined in Chapters 4 and 5. Because Wei Dan Gong is an advanced practice that works with various postures and visualizations, there are some additional considerations.

Dissolving the Energy Blockages

Relax with the breath. If you notice any sensation of tightness or 'burning' of the muscles during practice, consciously imagine and feel the tension dissolve and drip down into the earth as you exhale. There should be no strong visualization or effort used here — only a detached awareness.

Adjusting the Stances

Special attention should be focused on the alignment of the stances. If you are a student of the martial arts you should already have a good understanding of the stances. If you have no background in the martial arts, allow me to explain what stances are and their purpose.

A stance refers to the position of the feet and legs in a posture. Stances are the foundation that supports the upper body so they need to be firm, correctly aligned, and rooted. We are working with four stances in Wei Dan Gong Qigong: the Horse Stance (Holding the Post, Pressing Down the Earth, Holding the Baskets), the Front Bow and Arrow Stance (Holding Up Mt. Tai), the Seven Star Stance (Play the Lute), and the Riding the Tiger Stance (Retreat to Ride the Tiger). In the early stages of Wei Dan Gong stance work, a common occurrence is to experience the muscles and joints quickly becoming fatigued and sometimes shaking. The lower the stance, the more strain there is to work through. For this reason Wei Dan Gong uses medium to high frame stances that are more suitable for most people.

Another important consideration in stance work is the position of the Kua. Generally the term Kua refers to the area of the body where the upper part of the legs meets the torso. In a Wei Dan stance the Kua can be either open or closed and can affect the way the energy flows from the legs into the upper body. In the Horse

80

Stance both Kua(s) are open. In the Front Bow, Seven Star and Ride the Tiger Stances, one is open and the other is closed. Opening and closing the Kua is directed by the position of the waist. The position of the shoulders and hips aligns the waist.

Stances should never be "static." During your practice there is some degree of flexibility in shifting and adjusting your stances and postures as needed. Once you become more experienced in your Qigong practice, these adjustments will be reduced.

Chapter 7

Movement Wei Dan Gong Qigong

Movement Wei Dan exercises are much more dynamic than the stationary standing Qigong methods and help perfect the same energetic principles found in the Taijiquan solo form — correct body alignment, coordinating the movements with the breathing, and focusing the mind. These exercises also teach Taijiquan practitioners to recognize and sense the interplay between the two polarities of yin and yang within the movements and transitions of the postures.

In each movement or transition of Taijiquan, or Taiji Qigong, there is always some combination of yin-yang pairs in motion — simultaneously. Primarily yin-yang pairs are in the waist. Certain portions of the body are relaxed while other parts are energized by internal or external movements. However if the body is too relaxed without becoming energized it becomes too yin with insufficient yang to balance it. Conversely, physical exercise alone often causes the body to tense up (all yang and no yin), relying heavily on physical strength (Li).

Ideally, Movement Qigong should include both internal and external methods in order to insure a balanced energy training program. It should be noted that relying exclusively on isotonic (muscle tensing/relaxation) components of Qigong exercises can be more detrimental to your energy development than beneficial.[34] The Taoist masters would say that *with this type of training, there is no longevity,* meaning that people who work exclusively with this external technique do not

---

[34] For example, Iron Shirt Qigong which includes external body conditioning with weights, striking the body with mallets, and soaking the body in toxic herbs to toughen the skin.

receive very many positive health benefits from their practice and in extreme cases these practices may actually shorten their lives.[35]

The goal of Wei Dan Gong Movement Qigong is to harmonize Qi, increase flexibility in the muscles and joints, increase physical endurance, improve mental focus and to develop a sense of active Peng Jin. Peng Jin is the Chinese martial art term for Ward off or Guardian power — it is the mother energy intrinsic to all the postures of Qigong and Taijiquan. For those people who are not involved with martial art training, the concept of Peng Jin is equally important and can be thought of as the means of developing balance, poise and calm.

Qigong Opening Salutation

To begin Movement Wei Dan Gong practice it is good to first establish a strong energetic connection with the Three Materials (Heaven-Earth-Human Beings). By doing this, your body. mind, and spirit will be much more receptive and better able to assimilate the newly acquired energy.

Immortal Embraces the Universe Instruction

1. Preparation: Stand with feet shoulder width apart, arms relaxed at your sides. Posture erect (head up, back straight, knees slightly bent — (Figure 24A). Bring your arms out away from your body with the palms facing downward. (Figure 24B).
2. Inhale and raise both arms up the sides of your body with palms facing down (as if they are attached to the earth). Continue raising hands until the arms are held up over your head (elbows about shoulder level) with palms upturned towards the sky to receive the Heavenly Qi (Figure 24C). To complete the opening, reach upward and place palms together by first touching the little fingers — ring fingers — middle fingers — index fingers — thumbs, then palms together (Figure not shown).

---

[35] Muscle/Tendon Changing exercises only make you powerful in the short term. In regards to longevity, an ancient Taoist adage says that "if you die at 100 years of age, you died young."

3. As you exhale, slowly bring down palms and position them in front of the heart (Figure 24D).[36]
4. This posture (Figure 24D) represents the beginning of the interaction of the yin/yang energies that begin to move and rotate at the center — the creation of Taiji (Tai Chi).

Figure 24A: Immortal Embraces the Universe Step 1

---

[36] This posture represents Liang I the combination of the two polarities of yin and yang inherent in mankind.

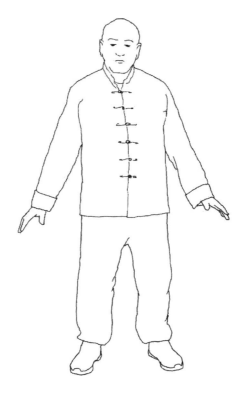

Figure 24B: Immortal Embraces the Universe Step 2

Figure 24C: Immortal Embraces the Universe Step 3

Figure 24D: Immortal Embraces the Universe Step 4

Wei Dan Gong Movement Qigong Instruction

Crane Flies Up to the Sky

1. Begin standing in Right Empty (Cat) Stance holding the Qi Ball (Figure 25A). Exhale through your nose as you proceed to step 2.
2. Crane Reaches Up — Right (Figure 25B): Step up with your left foot. Inhale as you reach upward with your right hand, palm up (gathering Qi through the palm, PC-8). As you reach up your weight shifts forward slightly raising the right heel. Simultaneously, the left arm reaches back with the palm turned upward. *Do not over extend your reach. Keep it comfortable.* As you exhale shift your weight back on to your right leg (about 80%). Hands form a ball by bringing the back arm around to the front of your abdomen and right palm down to form the top of the ball. *Try to keep the left palm facing upward as if you are holding a precious liquid that you don't want to spill out.* Repeat 8 to twelve times.Left Cat Stance (Figure 25C): Transition.Change sides by stepping back with the left foot (weight 80% on left leg), simultaneously roll the ball with the left hand on top of the ball.
3. Crane Reaches Up — Left (Figure 25D) is a mirror of steps 2 and 3. Repeat eight to twelve times.
4. Closing exercise: Return to the Source (Figure 26)

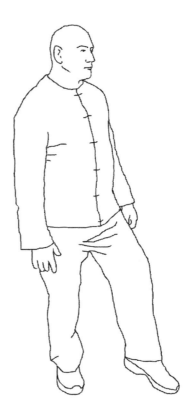

Figure 25A: Right Cat Stance

Figure 25B: Crane Reaches Up — Right

Figure 25C: Left Cat Stance

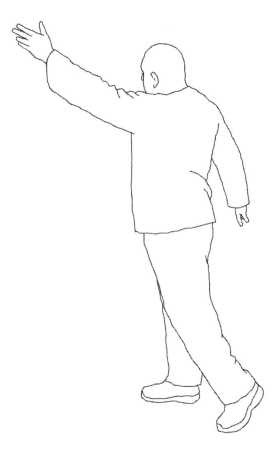

Figure 25D: Crane Reaches Up — Left

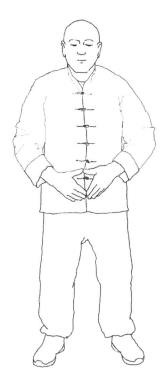

Figure 26: Return to the Source

Crane Opens Wings

1. Begin in standing posture, feet shoulder width, arms relaxed at your sides, head up, back straight. Tongue lightly touches the upper pallet behind the front teeth.
2. Facing front — exhale through the mouth, with the tongue neutral while dropping down into a Horse Stance — pressing down in front of your body with your palms (Figure 27A).
3. Inhale with tongue on upper pallet while opening arms outward as if you are inflating a big ball of energy (Figure 27B). *Your gaze follows the level of your hands, looking into infinity at the horizon.*
4. As you exhale, press down with both palms returning to Horse Stance (Figure 27A). Repeat steps 1 and 2 three times.
5. Continuing from Figure 27C. Inhale as you raise up out of Horse stance turning your body and opening out your arms to face the left corner (Figure 27D).
6. Return to horse stance (Figure 27C).
7. Continuing from horse stance (Figure 27C), inhale while raising up from horse stance and turning your body towards the right corner and opening out the arms. *Weight is on the right foot, and the left heel lifts up* (Figure 27F).
8. Return to Horse Stance (Figure 27E).
9. Repeat steps 3, 4 and 5 three times.
10. Closing: From Horse Stance (Figure 27E), bring feet to shoulder width apart and stand. Perform Return to the Source.

Figure 27A: Horse Stance

Figure 27B: Crane Opens Wings

Figure 27C: Horse Stance

Figure 27D: Crane Opens Wings Left

Figure 27E: Horse Stance

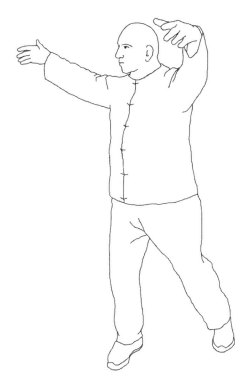

Figure 27F: Crane Opens Wings Right

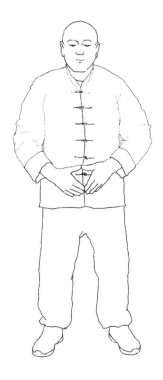

Figure 28: Return to the Source

Monkey Rolls the Ball

This exercise is energetically similar to classic Taiji Wave Hands in Clouds, in which the weight shifts from side to side as the waist turns. The breathing should be coordinated with the movement.

1. Begin with feet shoulder width and bring up arms and form a ball with the hands the left hand on top (Figure 29A). Weight evenly distributed on feet.
2. As you inhale, turn your waist to the left while holding the ball — shifting your weight to the left foot (Figure 29B).
3. Once you arrive at the right weight, exhale and turn the ball over - bringing your right hand to the top (Figure 29C).
4. Inhale, turning your waist to the right holding the ball and shifting your weight to the right foot (Figure 29C). Exhale while turning the waist and shifting your weight to the right foot (Figure 29D).
5. Turn over the ball (Figure 29A) and repeat the sequence by alternating sides twelve or more times
6. To close this exercise, return to center posture. Bring your hands down and perform Return to the Source.

Figure 29A: Monkey Rolls the Ball Step 1

Figure 29B: Monkey Rolls the Ball Step 2

Figure 29C: Monkey Rolls Ball Step 3

Figure 29D: Monkey Rolls Ball Step 4

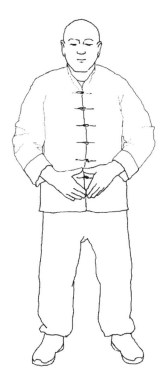

Figure 30: Return to the Source

Pushing the Circle

This exercise is a Taoist variation on the Shaolin Wei Dan exercise: Stirring the Cauldron, which develops the same set of martial skills. The only difference is the position of the hands. The Taoist version has both the arms held out with the palms facing down, and in the Shaolin version, the hands are formed into fists as if holding a ladle to stir a big pot of Jook.[37] The Shaolin exercise utilizes isotonic pressure while the Taoist version does not.

Begin by stepping into Left Bow Stance, left foot forward. Bring up the arms to about shoulder level keeping the shoulders and elbows relaxed — the elbows should not be locked and the shoulders not hunched up. Arms will remain in this position throughout the exercise (Figure 31A).

1. Inhale as you shift your weight back to a 60/40 (Empty Stance). *Do not lean back or allow the butt to stick out* (Figure 31B).
2. Exhale as you shift forward — using your waist to move your hands and arms in a clockwise circle shifting back to the Figure 31A posture. Inhale and shift back into Figure 31B. Repeat sequence 6 times.
3. Reverse the direction of the circle to counter-clockwise and repeat circling movement six times.
4. Switch sides — weight shifts to right front foot (Figure 31C) on the exhalation and to the left back foot on the inhalation, first circling counter-clockwise then clockwise (Figure 31D). Repeat the circling movement six times.
5. Closing exercises: Return to the Source.

---

[37] Jook: A thick rice congee or soup.

Figure 31A: Pushing the Circle Left Bow Stance

Figure 31B: Pushing the Circle Empty Stance

Figure 31 C: Pushing the Circle Right Bow Stance

Figure 31D: Reverse Pushing Circle Right Bow to Empty Stance

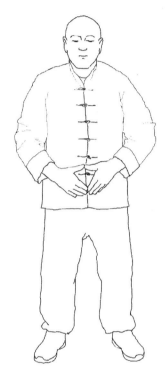

Figure 32: Return to the Source

After you have concluded the closing exercises following Wei Dan Gong and Movement Qigong practice, you are now primed and ready to begin a more rigorous workout. If you are not a martial artist and are not practicing forms and weapons, a good alternative is to simply go for a walk or jog. Taiji Qigong will be more effective if you follow practice with some form of light aerobic exercise to help stabilize your energy.

Chapter 8

Conclusion

I have presented the fundamental principles and the basic instructions for practicing Taiji Qigong. Now is the time to put them into practice. These exercises were originally designed for students of the internal martial arts (Taijiquan in particular) to enhance their martial abilities. However, you do not necessarily need to be a martial artist to enjoy practicing Taiji Qigong and benefit from the positive effects and increased personal vitality.

Self-discipline

"We have met the enemy, and he is us (Kelly). *"*

To make reasonable progress, it is necessary to overcome the limitations and restrictions we place upon ourselves. Try to be as consistent as possible with the time and place you practice. If you are unable to keep to a set schedule, do not worry — practice when you get the time. Approach your practice cheerfully and mindfully — don't become frustrated. Do not allow yourself to be distracted by outside commitments or problems.

When to Practice

The most difficult part of starting any kind of practice is deciding when to begin — the first step of any journey is always the hardest. Once you feel you're ready to apply some serious effort to learning Taiji Qigong, choose a time to practice that will work within your daily schedule, or you can simply practice anytime you have at least 10 to 15 minutes of free time that you can practice without interruptions. This amount of time should allow you the time to practice the opening warmup exercises, Basic Zhan Zhuang, and a short closing set. Once you are proficient with the basic exercises and you feel that you are ready to learn more, you may then proceed to Wei Dan Gong and Movement Qigong exercises.

A commonly asked question I get from my students is: "how long do I need to practice Qigong to begin feeling its benefits?" Some people begin to feel better the first time they practice. Other people who are in relatively good physical condition usually notice the positive benefits sooner than people just beginning to get back into shape. Most people will begin to notice that they are becoming more energetic and mentally alert after a few weeks or months. Be patient and allow your body to develop naturally and the benefits will follow. Remember that the body takes time to adapt to the increased energy. Increase the duration of your practice gradually. In the early stages of practice, do not try to practice any longer than a few minutes per session. Never practice with the expectation of effects. Avoid forcing your breathing or visualizations.

Once those exercises are learned you may begin working through the levels of refinement.

Levels of Achievement

Students who wish to achieve a higher level of achievement in their Qigong training need to begin building a strong foundation in Qigong theory and the underlying principles taught in the Taoist classical literature. The principles of the Tao Te Jing and Yi Jing should be studied and applied on a regular basis in order to receive deeper insights into how to improve your lifestyle and Qigong practice.

If you are not studying under a qualified Qigong expert and wish to learn basic Taiji Qigong, be sure you follow the rules outlined in the above chapters before attempting to learn on your own. It is always best to have a qualified instructor available to help you through the rough spots of your practice. If there are no teachers available in your geographical area, practice the basics on your own and allow your intuition to guide you. Intuition can be a very powerful tool if you are approaching your practice with honesty and sincerity. There are eight recognized levels of achievement in Taoist Qigong training. Taiji Qigong works with the first four. The higher levels are for more advanced energy cultivation practitioners and would require learning directly under the supervision of a master practitioner.

Eight Levels of Achievement in Qigong Training

1. Introduction to the theories and methods of a safe and effective practice. The importance of correctly following the basic rules of Qigong are learned. Basic Qigong methods are taught. This level of practice conditions and prepares the physical body and establishes the proper foundation for advanced levels of practice.
2. Students begin working with regulating the breathing and mind. The breath and mind act as intermediaries between the physical and energy bodies, as well as our consciousness. This stage trains the Xin (heart/ mind) and helps purge the body of negative elements that interfere with energy purification.
3. After practicing on a consistent basis for a few months, the inner-alchemical process of the conversion of Jing into Qi begins. Students begin to work with the various energetic components of the body and begin to acquire a sense of the 'inner vibrations' that move through our bodies during practice. The physical and energy bodies must work together as a unit to make reasonable progress in this stage of our development.

117

4. Activating the meridian system. This level is achieved by systematically building a strong foundation in Qigong training. Students must be patient and allow the energy to develop gradually. The conversion of Jing into Qi at this stage is nearly complete.
5. Rejuvenation. Once the energy body is cleared of blockages, the Yang Qi begins to flow unobstructed throughout the body. The quality of the internal energy improves and nourishes the organs and tissues. Practitioners who have reached this level appear youthful and are physically strong. This stage requires a higher degree of moral virtue and ethics.
6. Attainment of the internal vibration. Practitioners begin to distinguish the various substances and functions of the body as vibrational frequencies. The mind and the internal energy are now linked, and we are able to move the energy at will. Students learn their true nature by direct experience and discover the true way of knowledge and that knowledge will lead to wisdom. Wisdom is a much more profound level of understanding that ultimately leads to enlightenment. Practitioners become much more aware of their body, internally and externally, and most importantly, the reality of our integration with Nature (Tao) and the Universe.
7. Conversion of Qi into Shen. Energy is refined to the point that it begins to nourish our consciousness. We begin to develop a mind-altering comprehension that spiritual traditions strive to achieve such as Spiritual Enlightenment, Buddhahood, Christ-consciousness, etc.
8. Conversion of Shen into Tao. Masters of this level have become integrated with the subtle origin and possess extraordinary abilities. Consciousness converts to emptiness (the return to the subtle origin — the supreme achievement.

Glossary

Acquired Qi: Qi acquired through the air we breathe, the food we eat and the liquids we drink. also called After Heaven Qi or Post-Natal Qi.

Bagua: Eight Diagrams or Trigrams of the Yijing. Also called the Eight Jins (expressions of energy): ☰ ☲ ☳ ☴ ☶ ☵ ☷ ☷

Bai Hui: Hundred Meeting Point. Acupoint (Du-20) situated on the crown of the head. One of the Five Opening points. Convergence point of the Du, GB, Bl, TW and Lv channels.

Chong Mai: Penetrating or Thrusting vessel.One of the Eight Extraordinary Vessels.Has a regulating effect on all 12 of the regular channels, the uterus, and reproductive organs. Also called "The Sea of Blood."

Cun: Unit of measurement used in Chinese acupuncture. 1 cun = the width of the end of the middle finger (approx. 2cm). Varies by individual.

Cultivation: see Taoist cultivation.

Dao-in (Dao Yin): Chinese yoga. An ancient form of movement and stretching exercises.

Dai Mai: Belt channel or meridian. Only channel in the body that runs horizontally. Particularly important for female reproductive functions.

Dantien: A general term for the lower energy field of the abdomen located between the navel and spine and approximately 1 cm above the perineum.

Dong-Qi: Active Yuan-Qi. The center of the body's motive energy located between Kidneys.

Feng (Wind) Breathing: Strong sound of your own breathing "like a bellows."

Gong Fu: Popular term for Chinese boxing. Commonly spelled Kung Fu.

Gong Sun: Acupoint Sp-4. Activating point for the Dai Mai.

He Gu: Acupoint LI-4, Heavenly Star Point used extensively in Acupuncture, Tui Na, Dao In and Qigong. Regulates Wei-Qi.

Hexagram: Used in the Book of Changes for divination and spiritual counsel, comprised of two trigrams (stacked one on top of the other) that denotes a certain energy arrangement or circumstance (fortune).

Jin: A term used in Chinese martial arts for the expression of energy or power in movement or in self-defense application.

Jin Ye: The vital fluids that are part of the Five Vital Substances: Jing, Qi, Shen, and Blood (Xue). Jin type fluids are characterized as Yang in nature, light, watery, and light and circulate in the superficial layers of the body; Ye fluids are Yin in nature, dense, heavy, and turbid and circulate rather slowly in the body's interior.

Jing Mai: Regular channel system.

Kua: A general term for the area of the body, where the legs meet the torso - often used in Taijiquan as a reference to the hip joints.

Lao Gong: Acupoint PC-8 located in the center of each palm. One of the Five Gates.

Lie Que: Acupoint Lu-7. Activation point for the Ren Mai.

Liu Ho Ba Fa Quan: Six Harmonies-Eight Methods boxing. Internal art system that predates Taijiquan.

Marrow: Chinese medicine considers Kidney-Jing and Post-natal-Qi to be the sources of marrow and is referred to as a one of the 'Six Extraordinary (Curious) Yang Organs' in the body. Marrow is stored in the bones and the Brain and in TCM is called the Sea of Marrow.

Nei Dan: Internal Branch of Qigong.

Nei Guan: Acupoint PC-8. Activating point for the Yin Wei Mai.

Neijia: The internal or soft branch of the martial arts that follow the tenants of the Yellow Emperor's Classic of Internal Medicine (Neijing).

Original Qi: See Yuan-Qi.

Pericardium: Tissue that surrounds and helps protect the Heart. Recognized more for its function as a channel rather than as an organ, in Chinese medicine.

Peng: One of the Eight Jin (Warding Off) of the Bagua ☰

Qi: Life Force, personal vitality, or breath. In Qigong Theory, the energy that makes up the entire universe.

Qi Jie: The blood vessels.

Qi Jing Ba Mai: Eight Extraordinary Vessels or channels.

Shan Zhong: Acupoint (Ren-17) located at the center of the chest.

Shen Mai: Acupoint Bl-62. Activates the Yang Qiao Mai.

Shifu: Chinese Martial Art term meaning the head of the family or teacher. Sifu in Cantonese.

Taijiquan: Grand Ultimate Boxing.

Tao: Literally, "the way or path."

Taoist Cultivation: Perfecting and developing the body, mind, and spirit through meditation, movement practices, and lifestyle changes (Yang Sheng) working towards the goal of longevity and enlightenment.

Tao Te Jing: The Way and the Power. The teachings of Lao Zi.

Te: Taoist term for virtue, as in the Five Virtues: Acceptance-Wisdom-Patience, Compassion, and Empathy.

Tian Gui: Sexual essence.

Tiao: To regulate or control.

Trigram: In the Yi Jing, used to symbolize certain elements or possibilities: see Bagua.

Triple Warmer: Alternative name for San Jiao.

Tui Na: Massage techniques used in Chinese medicine and self-massage.

Wei Dan: External Branch of Qigong.

Wei Guan: Acupoint TW-5. Activating point for the Yang Wei Mai.

Wei-Qi: The protective located between the skin and the muscles.

Wu Xing: The Five Elements or Phases.

Xi Breathing: Term for breathing that is soft and inaudible.

Xin: The Heart or emotional mind.

Xing Yi Quan: Mind-shape boxing. Internal martial art developed sometime during the Sung Dynasty.

Yi: The intellectual mind.

Yang Qiao Mai: Yang Heel Vessel. Regulates and balances upper and lower regions of the body.

Yang Sheng: Literally, Nourishing Life. Living a lifestyle in harmony with the rhythms and laws of the universe. Includes proper diet, exercise, moral character, meditation, etc.

Yang Wei Mai: Regulates the six regular yang channels. Controls We-Qi and helps protect the body's exterior.

Yi Jing: Book of Changes or Book of Zhou. The most ancient of the Chinese classical texts on cosmology, geomancy and spiritual counsel.

Yin Qiao Mai: Yin Heel Vessel. Has a similar function as the Yang Qiao Mai.

Yin Wei Mai: Controls Ying-Qi and regulates internal organs and blood.

Ying-Qi: Qi derived from nutrition.

Yong Quan: Acupoints (K-1) located in the soles of the feet.

Yuan-Qi: Original, Pre Natal or Before Heaven Qi that is the Qi we inherited from our parents and ancestors that determines our physical constitution. Qi in its primordial, or potential state before manifestation into the material realm of existence.

Zangfu-Qi: The Qi of the Five Yin Organs, and Six Yang Organs; each organ having its own energy signature, or frequency.

Zhao Hai: Acupoint K-6. Activating point for the Yin Qiao Mai or Yin heel vessel.

Zheng Qi: Upright Qi. Actually not one specific type of qi, rather it is a term for qi in the whole body working together to defend the body against pathological invasion.

Zhi: 1. In Taoist cultivation, term for internal medicine (elixir). 2. Will Power.

Zhou: One of the Eight Jin (Elbowing) of the Bagua.

Ziran: Literally "self so-doing." Going with the flow, following the way of nature.

Zu Lin Qi: Acupoint GB-41. Activating point for the Dai Mai.

Works Cited

Jing-Nuan, Wu, translator. *Ling Shu or The Spiritual Pivot*. University of Hawaii Press, 1993.

Kelly, Walt, et al. *The Best of Pogo*. Simon and Schuster, 1982.

Lao Tzu, et al. *Tao Te Ching*. Vintage Books, 2012.

MacGill, Markus. "Lymphatic System: Definition, Anatomy, Function, and Diseases." *Medical News Today*, MediLexicon International, 23 Feb. 2018, www.medicalnewstoday.com/articles/303087.php.

Maciocia, Giovanni. *The Foundations of Chinese Medicine: a Comprehensive Text*. Elsevier, 2015.

Ni, Maoshing. *The Yellow Emperor's Classic of Medicine: a New Translation of the Neijing Suwen with Commentary*. Shambhala, 1995.

Ni, Hua Ching, translator. *I Ching: The Book of Changes and the Unchanging Truth*. Seven-star Communications Group, 1994.

Pregadio, Fabrizio. "Taoist Alchemy: Neidan and Waidan." *Taoist Alchemy: Neidan and Waidan*, Golden Elixir Press, 2014, www.goldenelixir.com/jindan.html.

Qigong. https://translate.google.com/#view=home&op=translate&sl=en&tl=zh-TW&text=qigong.

Shih, Tzu Kuo. *Qi Gong Therapy: the Chinese Art of Healing with Energy*. Edited by Charles Stein, Station Hill Press, 1994.

Xingdong, Li, et al. *Essentials of Chinese Wushu*. Foreign Language Press, 1992.

Yang. https://translate.google.com/#view=home&op=translate&sl=en&tl=zh-TW&text=yang

Yang, Jwing-Ming. The Root of Chinese Chi Kung the Secrets of Chi Kung Training. YMAA Publication Center, 1995.

Yin. https://translate.google.com/#view=home&op=translate&sl=en&tl=zh-TW&text=yin.

Zheng, San Feng. https://es.wikipedia.org/wiki/Zhang_Sanfeng#/media/ File:Changsanfeng.jpg.

Appendix A

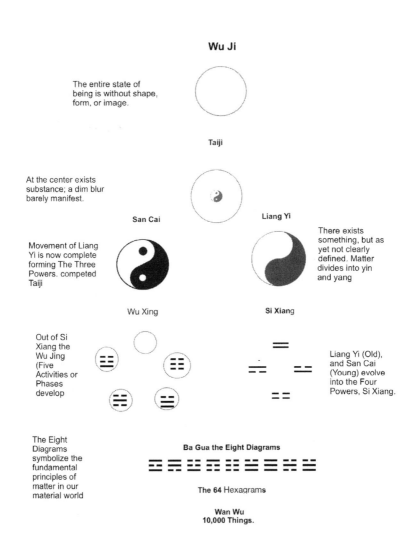

Wu Ji

The entire state of being is without shape, form, or image.

Taiji

At the center exists substance; a dim blur barely manifest.

San Cai

Liang Yi

Movement of Liang Yi is now complete forming The Three Powers. competed Taiji

There exists something, but as yet not clearly defined. Matter divides into yin and yang

Wu Xing

Si Xiang

Out of Si Xiang the Wu Jing (Five Activities or Phases develop

Liang Yi (Old), and San Cai (Young) evolve into the Four Powers, Si Xiang.

The Eight Diagrams symbolize the fundamental principles of matter in our material world

Ba Gua the Eight Diagrams

The 64 Hexagrams

**Wan Wu
10,000 Things.**

Source of Qi inHuman Physiology

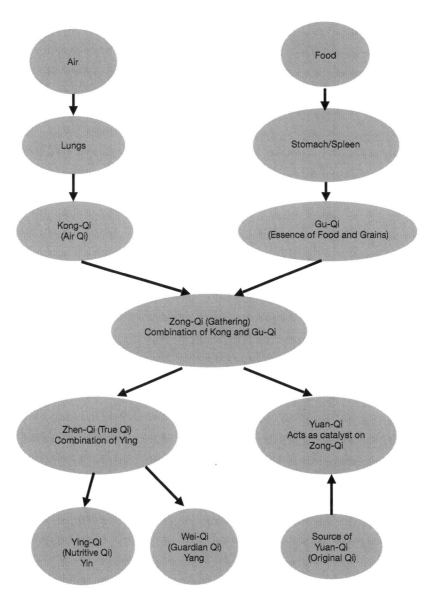

Made in the USA
Las Vegas, NV
16 January 2022